Flea markets in Europe

Flea markets in Europe

Jean-Claude Baudot ● Bernt Eberle ● Jan Halkes
Hans Jürgen Hansen ● Peter Hattink ● Ben Haveman
Alannah Hopkin ● Henk Huurdeman ● Paul Anton Keller
Wolfram Köhler ● Gerrit Overdijkink ● Norbet Paatsch
Peter Schatzmann ● Cees Straus

CHARTWELL
BOOKS, INC.

Published by
CHARTWELL BOOKS, INC.
A Division of **BOOK SALES, INC.**
110 Enterprise Avenue
Secaucus, New Jersey 07094

Library of congres number 81-68288

Copyright ⁽ᶜ⁾ 1982 Uitgeverij Van Dobbenburgh bv, Velp Holland.

ISBN 0-89009-499-3

Contents

The Authors
Jean-Claude Baudot: France
Bernt Eberle: Germany
Jan Halkes: Portugal
Hans Jürgen Hansen: Austria, Germany, Switzerland
Peter Hattink: Spain
Ben Haveman: Belgium, Netherlands
Alannah Hopkin: United Kingdom and Ireland
Henk Huurdeman: Belgium, Netherlands
Paul Anton Keller: Austria
Wolfram Köhler: Greece
Gerrit Overdijkink: Denmark
Norbert Paatsch: Germany
Peter G. Schatzmann: Germany
Cees Straus: Italy

Translated by
Col. N. Perkel Jr.
[Stichting Teksvterzorging, Amsterdam]

Photo Credits
AFP, Paris: 2, 22/23, 126
Igno Cuypers, Amsterdam: 109, 115
Peter Gnad, Graz: 54 below
Feddo van Gogh, Amsterdam: 107, 118, 119
Foto Körbel, Vienna: 54 above, 56, 57
George Hallett, Ille-sur-Têt: 26, 27
INBEL, Brussels: 91 above, 95
Evelinde Manon, Gräfelfing near Munich: 61, 64, 66, 68, 69 below, 72, 76/77, 77
Joop van Meurs, Waddinxveen: jacket, 80, 92/93, 96, 97, 100, 101, 104, 105, 112, 113, 116, 116/117, 120, 121, 124 below, 125, 128
Nordisk Pressefoto, Copenhagen: 86, 88
Manfred Olmer: 60
Norbert Paatsch: 73, 74
Marcella Pedone, Milan: 41, 44, 45, 48
Manfred Pfefferkorn: 81 above, 84
Photo Lohr, Graz: 53
Jan Roewer, Frankfurt on the Main: 69 above
E. & F. Schneider: 62
Karl Schweizer, Zurich: 59
David Simpson, Bisley: 29, 30, 32, 33, 129-133, 136, 137, 139, 140, 145-153, 157, 158
Stadt Nürnberg, Nuremberg: 81 below, 83
Süddeutscher Verlag, Munich: 78
Tom Weerheijm, Amsterdam: 43, 91 below, 98, 99, 102, 103, 122, 123, 124 above
Jacques Zekkar, Paris: 13, 16, 20, 21, 24

Intro

Whoever was it that said 'the times are a-changing'? Now it is no longer necessary to turn up one's nose at the idea of wearing an old dress in which once upon a time an old Sunday-school mistress walked about who suffered from one sort or another of skin complaint. Hanging up portraits of anonymous ladies and gentlemen is nowadays 'with-it', provided that the portraits are brownish and their frames oval-shaped, and that the collars or mustaches are old-fashioned enough. It is all in the times, and for this the flea market is responsible.

The flea market has also become a necessity, especially when one considers that there are, for example, record companies which are unable to get rid of their products, which then lie around as a blot on the world of commerce. As capitalist practice demands, these articles simply have to be dumped at a given moment, despite the fact that thousands and thousands of dollars are involved; just like tomatoes in Holland, or grapes in France. When this signal has been given, these products become worthless, even at the flea market – but here they will probably regain their value within a few years. This is the crux of the matter: flea markets are the last stop for the material remains of the objects which surround our lives before they are dumped into oblivion forever. Thus it may be said that the golden age of the flea market is upon us. Or, as a Frenchman would say: 'We're going to the fleas!'

The one talks of a 'flea market', the other of a 'lice market'. In Portugal one will need to ask for a 'thief-market' in order to find a flea market. But it all boils down to a place where all kinds of second-hand wares are sold. The phenomenon of this type of market has spread all over Europe like a plague of fleas during the last decades. The inevitable jump to the American continent was soon made, and cautious estimates now indicate some twelve hundred markets flourishing in the U.S.A. which are entitled to the epithet 'flea market'.

Markets have always been a big attraction for the public. Not only because of the reasonable prices, but also because of their festive atmosphere, haggling, smells, sounds of vendors and their casualness. With a dollar in your pocket, you can enjoy ten dollars' worth of entertainment. One need never be bored at a market, a unique phenomenon for a society that usually makes demands on the wallet for even the smallest of pleasures. For those who have an eye for detail and enjoy a more informal atmosphere than that afforded by the daily slur, the stalls and dialogues encountered at a market provide an experience which no amount of money can buy.

Surprisingly enough, little or no literature exists on this amazing phenomenon of the flea market. Perhaps it is because it is so recent.
But why 'flea market'?

The origin of the name 'flea market' is difficult to trace. In the time of Emperor Napoleon III, the imperial architect Haussmann made plans for the broad, straight boulevards with rows of square houses in the center of Paris, along which army divisions could march with much pompous noise. The plans forced many dealers in second-hand goods to flee their old dwellings; the alleys and slums were demolished. These dislodged merchants were, however, allowed to continue selling their wares undisturbed right in the north of Paris, just outside of the former fort, in front of the gate *Porte de Clignancourt*. The first stalls were erected in about 1860.

The first flea market of Paris grouped itself around two cafés, one called *Café de trois Canons* (Café of the Three Cannons), the other was on the Rue des Roziers. The 'puciers', as the merchants were called, acquired more and more territory, but however large the flea markets became, they always were in the close vicinity of a café where customer and seller could meet each other. The

gathering together of all these exiles from the slums of Paris was soon given the name 'Marché aux Puces', meaning 'flea market'. This term has nothing to do with the hygienic state of either the sellers or their wares and rests probably somewhere with middle class prejudice. A serious investigation into the origin of the name has not yet been undertaken.

France has some fifty flea markets at present, some open on weekends, others only a few times a year. England is a country with innumerable auctions and antique shops. Here the impoverishment of the nobility led to the ransacking of basements and attics full of goods. And in England, there has always been a passion for old things: the rich consider it a hobby, the poor a necessity.

In Germany, the flea market is a relatively new phenomenon. Here the 'Sammler Journal' keeps track of all the markets and informs the reader regularly of the supply. The magazine puts everything into map-form, and does not limit itself exclusively to Germany: places like Barcelona, Madrid, Vienna, Rome, Brussels, Amsterdam are also included. How else could a German know that in Groningen (Holland) much new copper is passed off as old?

Every country has something unique about its flea markets. In Holland, the sensitivity to the Sunday Observance Act led to a dispute about the Looiersgracht market. Apocalyptic vision of the market's possible closure incited heavy protests in which even government officials came under fire. Less protest comes the way of 'Comrade Walter', a German war-vet who palms off Nazi emblems at the 'Rastro' of Madrid with the aid of youths dressed in black.

On the left bank of the Maas River in the Belgian city of Liège, one can observe how 'militaria' has spread all over Europe like an infectious disease. In Hannover, Germany, railroad-officials' uniforms and other articles belonging to the world of the railroad determine the market happening.

If you buy *brocante* in the Swiss Le Landeron, you are doing your bit for the preservation of the old city-center to which much of market's proceeds go. Copenhagen's 'Loppetorv' is situated on Israel Square; but because this is merely a polite way of referring to a bare area, the Danes quickly rechristened it 'Sinai Desert'.

Market and fair are celebrated simultaneously by the Portuguese at their 'feiras', where one can usually buy locally manufactured products, while nearly everyone has heard of London's famous Portobello Road, which displays a bundling of all the characteristics of the numerous jumble-markets in Great Britain. The colorful, bizarre, fantastic Portobello Road has hundreds of stalls and stretches for some miles. Here Rolling Stone Mick Jagger bought his first penitentiary-type striped swim-suit, dating from the beginning of the century. At the Petticoat Lane market, vendors are famous for their conjuring tricks in word and gesture. This tourist attraction is of some size, but for some puritanical Englishmen, it is always an example of Sunday sacrilege.

A pleasant additional feature of flea markets is their location. They are often situated in picturesque surroundings, often nestling against the walls of an old church in an old city-center. Piety and the business spirit have always gone hand in hand through the ages, and tradesmen have seldom been able to complain as to the absence of beer-haunts in the proximity of the markets where deals could be toasted or, if necessary, drowned.

This is but a fragmentary depiction of the fascinating and almost endless world of Europe's flea markets. A more detailed description will follow, but first a question: who does buy things at a flea market?

Three groups can be immediately distinguished. Economic considerations compel many people to buy second-hand goods; particularly among migrant laborers this is a necessity. Secondly, students and other young people living in small rooms are also regulars at flea markets. But much larger is the third group, those who can afford to buy new things but who still prefer to comb the markets in search of a rarity, that 'special' object. Now what moves these people?

Perhaps it is simply nostalgia, a longing for a vaguely defined past, or maybe it has something to do with a growing aversion to our plastic society. There is also the desire to be 'different', to possess those articles which are no longer made, and which few people still have, such as furniture, books or clothes, which do not show the

marks of mass-production and which outlive both fashion and their owners. And these articles can be found in a world which hangs together by rags and wants no truck with the industrial designs of the influential renovators. This is the world of the flea market. It is not surprising that tourists from the ultra-modern U.S. are so desirous of articles from European flea markets. Shall we describe this as plundering, or as a desperate search for lost values?

It is also true that the flea market has become a necessity owing to the high cost of repairing broken-down appliances, which usually forces us onto the despised consumer merry-go-round. But doing it yourself does not mean you are competent, and so we need to go right on buying. It is also impossible to imagine the nostalgia for the plastics of our day which the coming generations may have. No-one who has consciously experienced the Secound World War could possibly have imagined that the objects of their hopelessness and despair would become some of the most sought-after articles of our day.

Why has this book been written? Numerous examples of Europe's flea markets and their wares will be provided and considering the growing interest in them, a guide through the color-ful, confusing maze of the flea market-world is hardly redundant. It is therefore a kind of handbook, containing maps, tips and other useful information. You will find some markets more elaborately described than others, but this is not a measure of their respective worth: some markets lend themselves to a more detailed treatment owing to their bigger diversity of goods or to their susceptibility to good anecdotes.

This book is not a price-catalogue. Fads and prices have a habit of being as jumpy as fleas and so an extensive catalogue of prices or supplies would only lead to unreliable information. Where prices are mentioned, it is only to aid the depiction of the atmosphere. That this book had to be an international guide is obvious, because tourism across a country border has become quite common. Secondly, this book has had a truly international compilation. Through the wonderful, fascinating world of the flea market, we, the compilers of this book who come from many different countries, will take you, the lover of antiques, the collector of special articles, the tourist who wishes merely to amuse himself or the expert on a host of things which are no longer made any more. To you we bid: 'Welcome to Europe' and... long live the flea market!

Additional info

Throughout this book are lists in which the most important cities which have flea markets are mentioned. These can also be found in their 'own' chapters; places in each country are listed alphabetically. In the chapter 'Great Britain and Republic of Ireland', the lists are moreover split up into districts owing to the large number of markets in these areas. Each market is marked with a black dot in order to facilitate the locating of them, even in cities which have more than one. The information given comprises the names of the markets, where and when they can be visited, and other items of interest. With France, Italy and Great Britain, post codes, districts and counties are noted after the place names in order to prevent confusion with places having the same name. All place names found in these lists are also included in the index at the back of the book.

Glossy shoes, horse-dung and strange people:
of 'puciers' and of bulging gold bosoms

France

Leave your boots at the gates of Paris. Some sounds Paris does not like. What is more, a pretty old song goes: 'When I walked through the streets of Paris emptying my bottle....'...leave your bottles too at the gates of Paris. Paris provides opportunity enough to dream. You need no bottles at all to move through this city. Anyway, my ramblings for today will not go beyond the gates. They are all wide open and therefore already excite our curiosity and oblige us to look boldly at that which is within. Moreover, every gate has its own air, smell and speciality. They are just like the many dishes that Paris brings to your foodloving minds. There is something for every taste, every palate, every inclination; for the epicure, the gourmet, or the glutton. If the automobile is your chosen form of transport, you will be able to admire all these gates one at a time as you constantly change clothes to suit what each gate demands that you wear: huge butcher's blouses at La Villette, checkered caps at La Chapelle or Montmartre, patent leather shoes at the Porte Dauphine.

Oh, the Porte Dauphine. Try entering Paris through this gate. While riding through the beautiful Bois de Boulogne, from the rural surroundings to the exciting atmosphere of the capital, you will have all the time you need to 'let off steam'. Porte Dauphine... stop right there.... Can you smell the aromas of rare liqueur, costly tobacco, tea from China or Ceylon, jasmine-colored Indian tea, or of perfume costing ten francs per drop evaporating from satin petticoats or rising from the two refined mouths of the old subway on both sides of the Foch Avenue? If your nose is just as sensitive as that of a setter, a cocker spaniel or a partridge spaniel of the highest pedigree in which the family traits have been well preserved, then you may just notice the subtle aroma of horse-dung, which was left behind by horses of the 'Second Empire', and is now lying steaming under the asphalt of one of the world's most elegant streets.

On either side of this gate is the Porte Maillot, with its roar of racing motor-bike engines, its musty smell of hot oil and gasoline, and the Porte Champerret, standing cautiously ajar so we may catch a glimpse of her Christian middle classes within; the Porte Champerret, with her whiffs of incense and Palais-de-Justice air, black and scarlet togas, priests, bishops and attorneys, where from plush doctors' rooms full of chrome and mahogany-wood, the clinking of scalpels sounds as they are pushed against one another.

We continue on our journey and because I think I know what it is you like, three gates will be given more of our attention than the others: the Porte de Montreuil, the Porte de Vanves and the Porte de Saint-Ouen. Imagine that you belong to those who work and who approach the city chiefly in the weekends as a 'tourist'. You need not feel bitter about this and do not harbor any bad feelings. These so-called days of rest are the perfect holiday for you who are a lover of second-hand goods, antiques and 'real finds'. You will not have a single minute to yourself... If you, like so many others, had come during the week, with your snazzy clothes in one half of your suitcase and denims in the other, then your jeans, apart from in a few 'in' bars for leftwing intellectuals, would not have been of much service to you. And if those you met were your friends, then you could meet them everywhere in Amsterdam, London or Berlin: they are primarily Europeans.

But the objects, furniture, toys, dolls, postcards and you name it, only come outside like sweet little kids on Saturdays and Sundays. Seeing that you have come to play with them, you must observe the rules. This will make the introduction a bit easier and so maybe friendships, even love, may come into being which will fill the trunks of your automobiles and take a choice place on their luggage-racks.

Friday evening. You have just arrived and, though you deny it, you are tired. Go to bed early after first eating in a peaceful, hospitable restau-

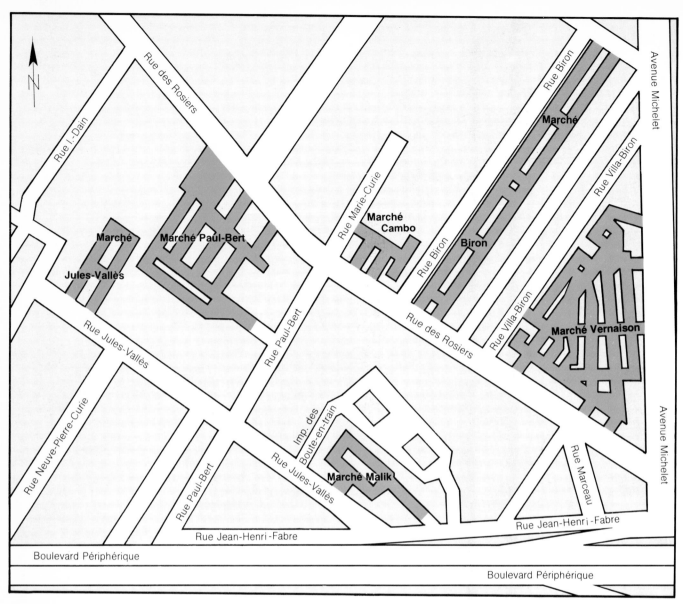

Paris
Porte de St. Ouen

rant. They are around. Then you ought to sleep.... until a quarter after six. Time to wake up, but not to the accompaniment of alarm-clocks going off: a few modest knocks at your door and hot croissants will start your day. Leave at about half past seven in the direction of Montreuil, leaving your automobile where it is. Take two empty suitcases for good luck and dive into the first available subway (metro). If it is especially pieces of furniture which you are after, and which, I have to admit, are difficult to carry under your arm, then you will have to pick them up later yourself at the risk of having to leave one of the members of your party behind as a deposit.... Eight o'clock: you have arrived... now be careful, you are not welcome. Do not talk too much, be quick and not too affable towards the dealers with whom you converse; act as if you are looking for something in particular.....and buy something completely different.

This is no charity bazaar here, with women of the world manning the stalls and buyers with big, sympathetic hearts; you are among pros, who are present especially amongst the buyers. This is the dodge: you have to act fast and decide real quick. Just tell yourself that a large number of 'customers' – an everyday name meaning the antiquarians from the French interior (read: provinces) and Paris – have come on this day to buy new wares for Sunday. They need only to discover that you are an experienced lover of secondhand goods, a collector or an aesthete, then watch out: in a split second they will have seen right through you. They will know what it is that turns you on and will bag it two lengths ahead of you. If this happens, you can only buy it back from them. It is what they are there for but unlike you, their meter keeps right on ticking, to put it bluntly, and the thing in which you were interested will rise in price with the ride, which

Above: *Glassware for the choosing*

Left: '*Alternative*'
*dealers in self-made
jewelry can also be
found in Paris.*

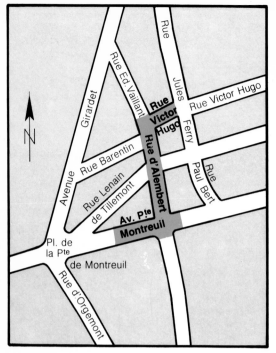

Paris
Porte de Montreuil

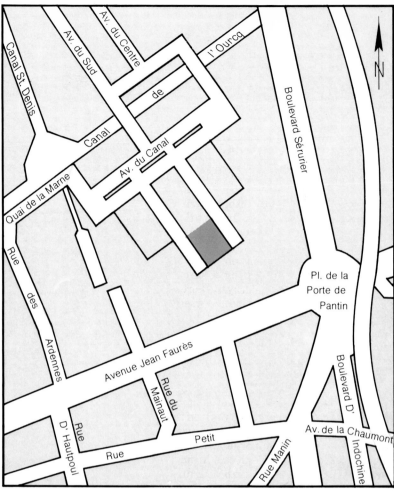

Paris
Porte de Pantin

is to say, by a pretty big profit margin. This is normal. Usually they will find more valuable and less damaged articles than you will. As they each have more or less their own speciality, they see to it that you do not waste time and that while trading you do not get, I will not say cheated, but to some extent conned; thus you can keep your hands clean.

Why then do we not approach them immediately? It is not my job to tell you that. It is the chase that does it. Some people give their preference to eating 'faisan sur canapé' in a five-star restaurant, others – and I will not permit myself to make any quality judgements – prefer to slaughter their own pheasants after trailing across the fields for hours and who, after these roamings, spend just as many admirable hours in binding, garnishing, tying up and dressing the birds as professional cooks do. Allow me to have the courage to be biased: the joy at a find on a sidewalk or amongst the junk of a stall has charms which are for me more inspiring than the love at first sight which a person necessarily feels towards an object which presents itself in front of his eyes, far from all outrageous practices, like the beautiful slave of his dreams on the

platform of the slave-trader.

But now to business: here you stand at the Porte de Montreuil, armed with the first piece of advice, the short introduction, which I have already given you. Now you have to know where to head for in order to give your buyer's talents full rein. The Porte de Montreuil is quite extensive but your hunting territory is somewhat more confined. A large part of it follows the ring-road which is not, in my opinion, the most interesting part of the market. Despite the early hour, the real professional dealers are already at their posts among the amateurs: all whose stores or sheds are situated in the neighborhood of this area, and there are many of them. We shall call them the 'puciers' of Montreuil, analogous to the 'puciers' of Saint-Ouen, who, as far as they are concerned, earned the title by being present and doing trade there for many years as professionals. You ought particularly not to avoid them, for two reasons: firstly, they have not yet gained the knowledge or the prestige of the dealers of Saint-Ouen; secondly, because there is not a single antiquarian or dealer in the world who has a monopoly on wisdom.

Whatever they look like, you will always be

able to find at these professional dealers an object which they do not know well and which you know better. But you can visit them later on in the day, because they will hardly leave the area before the following Monday and they are not the first to be looked up by dealers from elsewhere.

Head rather for the human beings who here and there are sitting or squatting in one of the semi-circles which are formed by the Porte de Montreuil itself. This showpiece is in itself quite exceptional; I hate using the word 'picturesque', which is supposed to give poverty something aesthetic. Poverty is never pretty but it is wortwhile to have to look at its terrible nature. Perhaps we are unable to do so with the eyes of a genius, like Eugène Suë or Victor Hugo, but at least we can become more aware of what it means to be poor. Do not believe yourself to be a benefactor if you have left your pennies with the amateurs who have survived the dare-devil search for bargains in garbage-cans, penurious attics or basements and old side boards full of personal possessions. Do not think badly of yourself either: they will, God be believed, very seldom have paid for what you buy from them and what is usually worth much more.

Strange characters walk around here, including outsiders, elderly beggars who are more or less sly, real paupers who are unable to make ends meet on their state pensions and sometimes even the occasional rogue. We shall not return to this group of people because you can find them at the same hour at any other jumble market. They differ per gate only in quantity.

Now you have to hurry. Whether you collect weapons, paintings, sculpture, old bronze or earthenware objects, there is always an antiquarian at hand who is also interested in these same objects. The collector has to depend on pure coincidence and quick decisions as he saunters around. Encourage yourself by thinking: I have to find here – and I am not the only one – at some dealer in postcards who comes from the rich suburbs, a thematic rarity which belongs to the most sought after: the vendor did not correctly estimate the value of that pathetic old lady among the old, dog-eared papers... and so on.

I once found a lovely steam locomotive of the make Radiguet dirt cheap, which a seasoned dealer had just found but which, according to

Aix-en-Provence (13)
● Place de Verdun, Tuesday, Thursday and Saturday morning

Angers (49)
● Place Louis Imbach, Saturday

Angoulème (16)
● Boulevard Berthelot, 2nd and 15th of the month

Annecy (74)
● On the bank of the Thiou, last Saturday of the month

Antibes (06)
● Thursday and Saturday

Argenteuil (95)
● Boulevard Héloïse, Sunday morning

Arles (13)
● Les Lices, Saturday morning

Audun-le Tiche (57)
● First Sunday of the month

Avignon (84)
● Place des Carmes, Sunday

Bayonne (64)
● Place d'Aine, Friday

Belfort (90)
● First Sunday of the month

Besançon (25)
● Place de la Révolution, Saturday morning

Béziers (33)
● Place du 14-Juillet (Champ du Mars), Friday morning

Bordeaux (33)
● Place Meynard, from Wednesday to Friday and Sunday morning

Bourg-en-Bresse (01)
● Place Carriat, Wednesday

Brive-la-Gaillarde (19)
● Place Molière, Boulevard Anatole-France, first and third Tuesdays of the month

Cavalaire (83)
● Wednesday morning

Chalon-sur-Saône (71)
● Place de Baune, Friday morning

Chartres (28)
● On the church square of the St. Pierre, Sunday

Chateauroux (36)
● Avenue des Marins, first Sunday of the month

Clermont-Ferrand (63)
● Place de la Liberté, first Sunday of the month from 8:00 to 18:00h and 11 May, 13 August and 9 November.

Colmar (68)
● Place de Marché aux Fruits, Thursday morning, mainly in summer.

Crevecoeur (93)
● Place de l'Hôtel-de-Ville, on Ascencion Day

Dijon (21)
● Place de la Banque, Tuesday and Friday morning

St. Etienne (42)
● Avenue Augustin-Dupré, Sunday morning

Grenoble (38)
● Second Saturday or Sunday of the month

Isle-sur-Sorge (84)
● Sunday

La Rochelle (17)
● Rue St. Nicolas, first and third Wednesday of the month

Le Mans (72)
● Avenue de Paderborn, at the foot of the cathedral, Friday and Saturday

Le Puy (43)
● Place du Martouret, Saturday and normal market days

Lille (59)
● Marché de Wazemmes, Sunday morning

him, was too good to be real. But it was, and it appeared afterwards to be absolutely genuine. I have also found tens of original 'Tintin' editions which seemed sooner dirty than authentic, and still....

Consider now that you have already seen the whole market and have profited from all the interesting offers; do not leave just yet. Go drink a cup of coffee first and trust the heavy suitcase to the barman.

Regardless of whether or not you can always find something a second time, have trust in coincidence, which is often a more worthy ally than serious searching. You can enjoy yourself to the full in the atmosphere which is just as rare, diverse and refined as the aromas emanating from a little stall selling all kinds of spices. You can find dealers who get rid of new materials or tools for a small sum, sellers of mens' suits who praise their models, which are of better quality than the suits of Lanvin or Ted Lapidus; fortune-tellers who scold you with a no less colorful profusion of

incantations, newspaper sellers who attempt to sell you the very last edition of the First World War, revised and corrected by a publisher of facsimiles, and art dealers in possession of more masterpieces than Mr. Pétrides himself. For prices varying between five and seventy-five dollars, they attempt to sell you a whole series of Picasso's, Braques, Rubens, Greco's and what have you, and of even more famous artists than these.

Then there are the cooks and pastry-bakers. Rancid cakes, french fries fried in batter, cream-cakes so old that they seem to have been sweetened with saccharine from the last war, bringing memories of those times to mind, are on sale here: think of Proust's Madeleine. The business in second-hand goods will even bring pleasure to your taste-buds and you can eat, strangely enough, without having to worry about the consequences. The products which you will consume are very seldom poisonous but their taste will make you recall a host of 'mom's apple-pie' me-

The nostalgic trend is enjoying golden times

Paris
Porte d'Italie

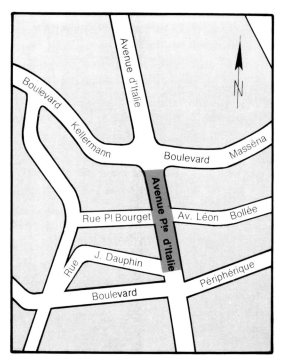

Marseilles
La Joliette

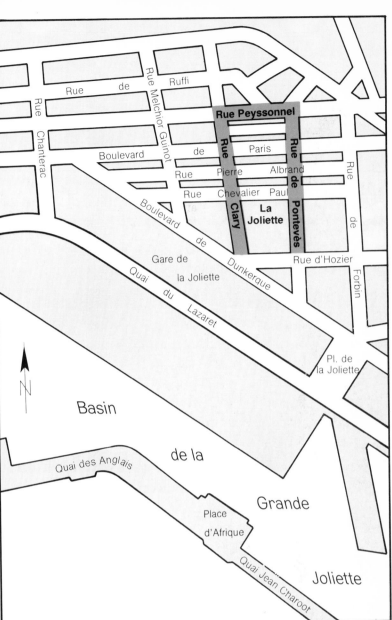

mories.

Assume now that, after all your searching, it is time for lunch. You will certainly find something in the same area to fortify your insides without your being served a real feast, which, in all honesty, you should definitely not expect. I advise you the following, unless you want to walk on to the Porte de la Villette or the Porte Pantin. About midday, you will see those individuals leaving the market who had been the immediate center of your interest during the morning and who were also the reason why I, stating my grounds, impressed on you to get up earlier than usual. You will see their places gradually being taken by other dealers, who reserve their pieces of the road weekly and who will have occupied them by about one o'clock.

And if you have only filled one of your two cases, after a visit to these guys you will have trouble getting the other one closed. Moreover, you will, if it is not objects with which you are primarily concerned, find a really large selection

Paris
Porte de Vanves

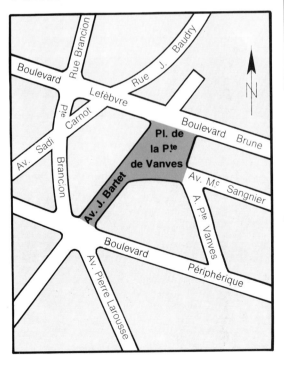

Flea markets Limoges-Montpellier

Limoges (87)
● Place d'Aine, Wednesday and Saturday

Lyons (69)
● Marché aux Puces de la Feyssine 1 bis, rue Joseph Mertin à Vaulx-en-Velin, Saturday and Sunday morning

Marseilles (13)
● Quartier St. Lazare: rue Peyssonnel, rue de Pontevés, rue Clary, Sunday morning

Metz (57)
● Place des Frères-Lacretelle, behind l'Hôpital Legouest, first and third Saturday of the month

Montauban (82)
● Place Prax-Paris, Saturday

Mont de Marsan (40)
● Halles Saint Roch, first Wednesday of the month

Montpellier (34)
● Place des Arceaux, Saturday morning

of rustic and more or less genuine pieces of Louis XIII furniture. In fact – and I mention this to defend those already in possession of them – I believe deep in my heart that no more authentic Louis XIII furniture is in existence. Be satisfied with the Louis XVI, Louis Philippe or Napoleon III styles: they will undoubtedly need to be restored but you can be sure that they are authentic. As far as the Charles X furniture goes or the furniture in the typical 1900 style (Marojel amongst others), these are so much in demand that you are advised to quicken your pace if you still want to find them. By definition, miracles happen seldom, however.

Really, after this your day will have been spent most fruitfully and if you intend to do something other than to stretch out drowsily on your more or less voluptuous hotel mattress, then you must have at your disposal the same sources of strength as the comrades of Mao Tse Tung had when they took part in the Long March.

Prepare your following day next. You will have to wake up at the same time and will have to eat red meat together with a fortifying old Bordeaux. I myself have to think involuntarily about other affairs, and there spring to mind of this 'old woman-hunter' (expression has nothing to do with that noble art of hunting big game) various names of establishments in which the 'girls of Paris' grow without even the smallest of leaves to protect their tender stems. But you are not reading this to hear about that.

And there you are, at the Porte de Vanves, at eight o'clock Sunday morning.

Here the atmosphere changes. Rest assured, among the buyers there are still antiquarians to be found but it is different with the sellers: there are relatively few experts among them. You will mostly come across the motley assortment of vagabonds whom you have already seen the previous evening; this explains the small amount of furniture for sale. And where are the pros then? They are certainly around but they do not deal in second-hand goods. They look more like market-hawkers and they sell just about the same kinds of things as those already mentioned who offer you their goods on the squares of the small provincial towns.

But you will have made good use of your time if you remain here for two or three hours. At about eleven o'clock you should leave again, more or less loaded up and settled down, and I advise you – your room will have been cleaned – to go back to your hotel. Wash your hands, which you will feel like doing, put a little eau de cologne on your hair or some perfume behind your ears, and now without any further ado: surrender to your sweet-tooth!

This area is famous for its gastronomical treats and with a little help from a culinary guide you will, whatever people may have said, discover those cheap diners or one of those temples dedicated to the kitchen, where people make more sacrifices to food than to advertising. You will also most probably come across a group of initiated customers in one of them. Good luck!

At about three o'clock, not having drunk too much, proceed on your way to Saint-Ouen... Saint-Ouen... despite everything, it is always something special to visit the largest antique market in the world. Indeed it is more difficult to come by real rarities here and the prices are higher. You will have to deal only with professionals, the famous 'puciers' (they invented the name). They are now excellent antiquarians, have been almost everywhere, are very much in the know about all the various collections, but because they have used the method too many times in the past, they are not keen on bargaining followed by cash-payments; they all have a bank account and money, and also something like a 'carpetdealer complex'. On the other hand, you will find far nicer things for prices which keep the mean between 'utterly outrageous' and 'perfectly reasonable'.

There are still five markets to be visited each of which has more or less its own speciality. The Biron Market is undoubtedly the most snobbish; at the 'Paul Bert' there is a bigger assortment; at the 'Vernaison' more furniture; at the 'Jules Vallès' more of all sorts of things; the Malik Market is the most luxurious, and all the sidewalks of the bordering streets are more in favor with collectors. Furthermore there are, of course, also about ten real big specialists, noble folk almost, whom you can find not only at the 'Biron' but also at the Malik Market, which is abundant in almost everything of interest to the lover.

But the wealth of Saint-Ouen is not yet ex-

18

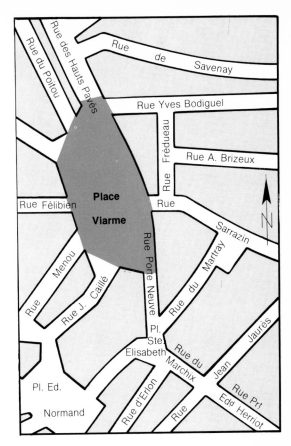

Nantes
Place Viarme

hausted and so I advise you not to concentrate too much on this characteristic aspect of the market on this particular Sunday but rather on her less important facets.

As everyone already knows, Sundays should be especially devoted to one's loving wife and darling children. So do not forget that a clothes-market is close at hand which is particularly in fashion and which is visited by the biggest snobs in the capital. Here are all kinds of things: from clothes worn in grandmama's day, useful for a weekend in Deauville in a Hispano-Suiza with supper in the Hotel Normandy, to clothes such as a well-dressed fortune-teller would wear, including lovely shawls and long dresses which are, depending on the district in which the parties are to be thrown, more or less transparent (the more classy the suburb, the more transparent the clothing: in the area of Neuilly, breasts are hardly covered at all). You will also find multi-colored blouses and, if you are exceptionally sophisticated, underwear that matches your outfit, from corsets to satin suspenders to garters from the 'Belle Epoque'.... But watch out! Choose carefully, there are more stalls with clothes from grandmama's day than with really old clothes. For the cold evenings there is a lot of fur, from fox-fur to mink. With a little bit of luck, all of these have once been worn by some famous celebrity from the film or show-biz world and have washed up here like silver-colored spangles from a mermaid washed up onto the beach. As far as shoes go, you will not believe your eyes: a fairy-tale prince would not find his Cinderella in any of these.

Back to our antiques. I have advised you not to pay too much attention to these, for the following reason, wich is based purely on my own opinion and so, as is only right, I offer it but tentatively: I have already told you that the flea market of Saint-Ouen is real pro-territory. They have been busy the whole of the previous week, out looking for buys, and they have completed their business-trips with a very early morning visit to the famous Porte de Montreuil and the Porte de Vanves, where you have already been, remember? On my advice, I hope. Mondays are a closing day for them – at least for those who sell their wares fast, even if they do thereby make less profit (and there are many like them): this is why

Flea markets Nancy-Paris

Nancy (54)
● Grande Rue, second Saturday of the month.

Nantes (44)
● Place Viarme, Saturday morning

Narbonne (11)
● Place Voltaire, Thursday

Nice (06)
● Boulevard Risso, Quai du Paillon Monday through Saturday

Nîmes (30)
● Rue Condé, Allée Jean-Jaurès, Monday

Orléans (45)
● behind the Eglise St. Paul, Place de la République, Saturday

Paris (Paris)
● La Porte Didot (Porte de Vanves), Saturday and Sunday
● Between Saint-Ouen and Clignancourt, Saturday, Sunday and Monday
● La Place d'Aligre, Tuesday through Sunday morning
● La Porte de Montreuil, Saturday, Sunday and Monday
● Bicêtre, Avenue Eugène-Thomas (Porte d'Italie), Tuesday, Thursday and Sunday
● Porte de Pantin, Marché des Greniers de France, Friday, Saturday and Sunday
● Postage Stamp Market: Corner of Avenue Gabriel and Avenue Marigny, Thursday afternoon, Sunday and holidays from 8:00 to 19:00h

right: *Laymen can have difficulty in distinguishing phony antiques from genuine ones.*
left: *Thousands of tourists visit the Parisian flea markets every year, but the local population is by no means redundant.*

21

The 'Vernaisson':
specialized in
furniture

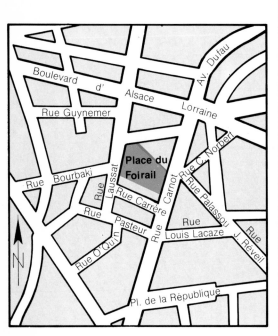

Pau
Place du Forail

Flea markets Pau-Perpignan

Pau (64)
● Place du Foirail, Saturday,
Sunday and Monday

Perigueux (24)
● Place Francheville, Wednesday
and Saturday

Perpignan (66)
● Avenue Leclerc, Place du Marché
de Gros (will probably be moved to
Marché Saint Charles at the edge of
the city) Sunday morning

you should visit them particularly on a Monday.
You will see that they let you 'bring them down'
more easily.

Well, well, I do not wish to say much more on
the markets of Paris. I have dealt with the interests of the 'collector-lover-antiquarian-
consumer' as well as with those of the rural
dweller or foreigner which you probably are.
This has been my way of saying: 'Welcome to
Paris!' Have a good look around, eat well, but
most of all, have a damn good time!

In any case, I am not quite finished with you: I
still want to discuss the few jumble-markets in
the old cities like Tours, Lille or Perpignan.

But I do not feel like leaving the Saint-Ouen
Market just yet. It is so important, so large, it has
inspired so many artists, musicians, painters
and poets, that we will, if it please you, return to
it once again. Let us not forget that, despite everything, it has, to my way of thinking, just as
many attractions for the tourist and for those
who share my interests as the Butte Montmarte,
the Champs Elysées, Pigalle, Notre Dame, the
Casino de Paris or Maxim's. Having finished
talking about this market, I always get the idea
that I have been too brief. As far as that goes, I

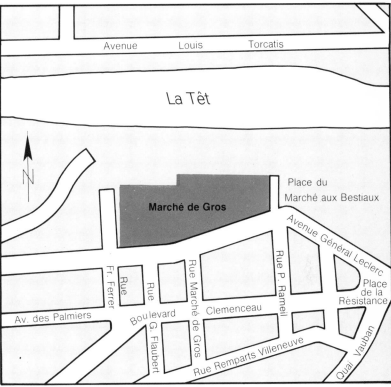

Perpignan
Place du Marché de Gros

end up behaving like those speedy tourists who always think that they have missed something. They go back to the market just to make sure they have nothing to reproach themselves for, as if they wished that the old 'maîtresse' had not yet told them the most important things and that it was still possible to talk to her.

I have already told you about the 'Biron' and the 'Malik' and their neighboring streets whose sidewalks are decorated with various curiosities amongst which you can wander over and again, despite the irregular working hours of the exhibitors, with the certainty that you will find every time a large number of objects which you had missed at a first glance.

You can find there then a large number of trains, dolls or lead soldiers, which escape the attention of the vendors and which, if they can take advantage of the inattentiveness of the vendor, 'lead their own lives'. Everyone knows – and we knew it long before Anderson told us – that some toys constantly follow their own minds; marriages are consecrated in sewers between proud dragoons and dancers in ballet-suits, without our seeing or the Church coming into the act; that suddenly ships begin to sail at

full speed carrying pirates on board who are in search of a treasure which is lying concealed at the corner of a sewer between old newspapers.

Gee whizz! In my ecstasy I notice that my enthusiasm has made me forget that I have not yet talked to you about the other markets which are also very important: the 'Vernaison' and the 'Paul Bert'.

For forgetting the 'Vernaison' I undoubtedly have an excuse: there is particularly a surplus of furniture here and, as you have probably noticed, my pecadillo consists of the unconditional attraction to all kinds of odds and ends. I often forget, quite egotistically, that some of you have come with pick-ups or automobiles with excessively large trunk-space or with firmly mounted luggage-racks on the roof. For you, the 'Vernaison' is the perfect feast.

I remember that, in the sixties, I once bought here a strong, giant, oaken chest of drawers, wich was not only rustic, but which was also genuine Louis XV. It cost me the sum of sixty dollars. For about three months, I blamed myself for the purchase every time I thought of my pretty blond kids whom, if I had been a little less egotistic, I could have propped full of chocolates,

23

Above: *Care in buying a ring*
Left: *Much attention for small things*

clothes or shoes, for the same amount of money. I also found the price too high for a piece of furniture of that size for which there is no space in a normal apartment. When at last I had brought it under the roof, I found, moreover, that it did not have enough character. Having placed the chest between two large showcases full of leaden soldiers, I blamed it for relegating my dearly-loved collection to the background without the slightest display of tact. After regret came hate. I can assure you that for ten years I led an unpleasant life because of my too spontaneous purchase and that for all this time we had as unpleasant a relationship as Paul Jouhandeau and his wife.

Fifteen years later, I managed to sell it, by a huge stroke of luck, for the price of one thousand dollars. There was not even a moment's question of bargaining, because the price was absolutely reasonable!

Yes, you can do good business here, if you do not have the luck, nor nurture the desire, to turn every love into a marriage, regardless of the price that may cost you. I can guarantee that the Breton or Normandy cupboards, the sideboards from Savoy or the desks from Elzas are generally sold for less money than at the places they come from.

Why is this? You should never forget that the big 'pucier' is a brilliant buyer and that his approach can often spare you much fruitless mileage.

While you are negotiating over many space-consuming purchases, your family members of the fair sex can have their fill at stalls selling all kinds of buttons. They are a kind of time-forgotten thread and ribbon store where horns, mother-of-pearls and silver buttons dating from the eighteenth century until the present day can be bought.

There are also shells and minerals; it is just as if you are on a sandy beach in the Bahamas or as if you have just climbed a thousand yards up a steep cliff, with the aid of a rope, and arrived at a

24

Strasbourg
Place de l'Hôpital

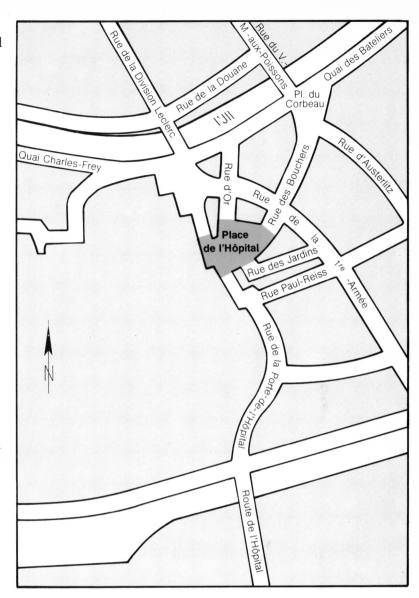

crystal palace.

While they still lived, one could meet Vilmorin and André Malraux here. I am convinced that they found here at least a quarter of their fairy-tale collections, which matched very well the extremely rare objects that our author/adventurer had brought back with him from the East. His pockets were always filled with prohibited articles, some of which he is sure he lost at the Angkor Temple.

As far as the 'Paul Bert' goes, this is a paradise for lovers of objects dating from 1900 tot 1925 consisting of ballerinas made of porcelain, women of light morals attached to powder-puffs on which the powder is still present and beautiful, exotic images. There are also little statues which represent warriors, war-loving horsemen, or, should the warrior want something more peaceful, lovely girls whose breasts are bare. You will be able to see all the odds and ends which our parents and grandparents loved: whole collections of more or less decorated boxes, pipes, copper lamps inlaid with fake precious stones and with diamonds larger than the 'Régent'.

And now to the provinces...

I deliberately begin, on the strength of the most complete bias, with the flea market of Narbonne. The sun is usually shining there. I myself prefer to go treasure-hunting in a fair climate than to hunt in far-off, heavily snow-covered regions for the 'treasure' – as far as it ever existed – 'of the Knights of the German Order'. And I am not the only one: witness the song by Gilbert Bécaud on the markets of the Provence.

Whatever wares people may sell here, we find ourselves in the country of the 'Langue d'oc' (the language which used to be spoken south of the Loire). The aromas in this country come from the 'garrigue', the shrub-like vegetation which one comes across in the Mediterranean regions and which is spread by rabbits with paws smelling of thyme.

Now allow me to let you in on a secret... One day in August 1977, I found an excellent starting-point to a collection of which the best pieces now decorate the radiator-grills of my automobiles from the beginning of the twentieth century. I am talking about the ornamental caps for the water-reservoirs which used to decorate the hoods of those modern vehicles: women with

Flea markets Reims-Strasbourg

Reims (51)
● Avenue Jean Jaurès, Sunday morning

Rennes (35)
● Boulevard de la Tour-d'Auvergne, Friday, Saturday and the normal monthly market days

Roubaix (59)
● Place de la Halle, Saturday and Sunday from 9:00 to 12:00h

Rouen (76)
● Place des Emmurès, Wednesday
● Near Saint Marc, Saturday

Seine-Port (77)
● Place Centrale, first Sunday of the month

Strasbourg (67)
● Place de l'Hôpital, Wednesday and Saturday

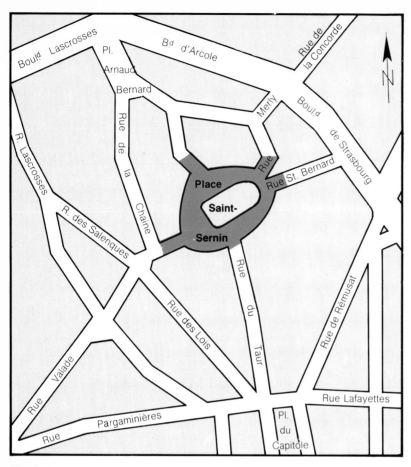

Toulouse
Pl. Saint-Sernin

Below: *The Arab residents at the Perpignan flea market form the largest group of buyers, especially of clothes*

Old pictures are much in demand

Flea markets Tarbes-Valence

Tarbes (65)
● Place Marcadieu, Thursday

Thionville (57)
● Extension of Rue du Manège, Place de la Liberté, second Saturday of the month

Toulon (83)
● Place Pasteur, Sunday morning

Toulouse (31)
● Near Basilique St. Sernin, Saturday, Sunday and Monday

Tours (37)
● Place de la Victoire, Friday morning and Saturday morning

Troyes (10)
● Place Saint Rémy, Saturday morning

Tulle (19)
● Quai de la Corrèze, Wednesday and Saturday

Valence (26)
● Place de la Pierre (Place Belat), first Sunday morning of the month

round breasts pointing at the horizons, the beautiful deer in the fanciful forests of Chrysler and the fairy-tale unicorns... All bought dirt cheap.

But take note: on the other hand it is a fact that the inhabitants of Languedoc are well-educated. Here you will not be able to find cheap piles of precious books such as you may find in some of the less intellectual areas of our so witty fatherland. Furthermore, it appears that the poetry of this region does not get on at all well with what I shall call the morbid surrealism, which one comes across often in our provinces where chilly, clammy superstitious habits are still deeply rooted. Once a Mohammedan hermit, always one. And if you want him to look like a mandrake, you have to go firstly to the Atlantic Ocean, sail via the Channel to the north and then go on land on some North Sea beach or other. Such is also the case with erotica, which is a luxury article in cold countries, originating from a longing for the naked flesh, where light, perfumed lingerie has become, with unlimited fantasies, a fetish.

As far as the market at Tours goes, this was, and still is, a treasure trove for the antiquarians from Paris and even from Upper and Lower Normandy. If the Loire delighted our kings, whether they came from the Guises lineage or that of the Valois, if the climate is mild, the forests cool and maybe enchanted, then it is thank to the mortal remains of our minstrels which are lying under the fertile ground here and who, with their songs, gently rock the somber burial-places of those heroes who died in the Champagne Pouilleuse, the Marne, the Somme or Verdun.

There is some of everything here and rest assured, there is also furniture which is becoming less and less common outside of the mountainous regions like Savoy of the Jura. This furniture is to be found in middle-class or aristocratic houses and not on rich farms or in handily remodelled cabins. You will also find here much gilding and precious veneering and fine, round frameworks.

As far as old jewelry goes, it is true that there is less to be found in Blois since the wild poaching expeditions, which the Amazons regularly undertook, with their bosoms bulging with gold; but really, there is still some left over... The jewels are undoubtedly not very valuable or

Even a vendor has to eat

precious but they are just as refined and extravagant as ever...

Regarding the market in Lille, you should go there in large numbers and show a preference for male business: it is namely a paradise for lovers of armaments and really old tools. You can find iron crosses, which are hung from old weaving-looms, bayonets and maybe, if the Gods of the North favor you, those old copper mine-lamps, which, just like their carriers, have remained under the ground as a result of a terrible explosion.

And thanks to Zola, some equipment remains from those brave men who journeyed to the center of the earth and who, with the aid of the strong ropes of Jules Verne's balloons which were rigged for space-exploration, were raised unto the light.

I have chosen three cities to discuss now. But France swarms with flea markets, like Strasbourg, Rennes, the large street-fairs of Normandy, Nancy or Aix-en-Provence. They compete with one another or melt together into one market. At these markets one can hear every accent and every dialect is spoken. You will also find well-filled shoulder-bags full of souvenirs, because people have gotten used to travelling since the time our companions had to make a trip through France. Only by the leather can it be seen where the bags are from.

'Camarada Walter's' fascist greeting,
a Sunday fury in the puppet-theater
and: how sticky are pepitos at the Rastro?

Spain

The streets of Madrid's 'Rastro' are the open lobbies of the Spanish United Nations. Gypsies, Spaniards, Arabs, Jews, Hindus, Vietnamese, Chinese, Europeans and negroes mingle in a brotherly fashion at the colorful flea market, which is protected by a statue of the Spanish soldier Cascorro. As the Spaniards themselves say: 'At the Rastro, more than two thousand years ago, Christians and Moors, thieves and policemen, and true and false prophets declared a truce.'

The small square at the beginning of the 'Rastro', the Plazza de Cascorro, named after the hero of the previous century but actually called the Eloy Gonzalo García, has been the barometer of what lives or could live in the hearts of Madrid's citizens, since times gone by. If it was, in the time of Franco, a gathering place for automobiles, which reflected the Spanish economic wonder, now it is a mini-center of political propaganda. In the stalls, the parties sell their ideologies, which fly over the counter like hot cakes, all under the watchful eye of Cascorro. Because Spanish cakes are sometimes sold too hot, the aged Cascorro enjoys the support of some police agents, who see to it that the stalls are not wrenched from their political context.

Talking about cakes: everyone who wanders around the 'Rastro' on a Sunday eats the traditional 'pepito', also called 'relleno'; a cold, candied cake with a cream filling. With a 'pepito', you still are given a piece of paper to keep your hands from getting sticky, because Latin negotiating always involves slaps on the shoulder and handshakes. And you can't do that with sticky hands. So one eats cakes in the sun while looking for something antique or some other junk. Olé!

'Olé' reminds one of bullfights. At the 'Rastro', there is space for the foreign hero who wants to surprise his family. 'Put your name here', on a Spanish poster, between the names of famous bull-fighters. Between Benito El Cordobes and Paco Camino, there is suddenly Joe Johnson from Nashville Tenn. Ah, what the hell, why not? It is better than the name Jane Wallace between the names of Alfonso Alvarez Jiminez and Pedro Sanchez Gil on a Spanish poster with the life-size heading 'R.I.P.', which comes from a stall that the public chuckles at rather than buys from.

The 'Rastro' has something legendary about it. It begins at the subway exit Tirso de Molina, which, unlike the underground in Paris, preserves the solid, old-fashioned steel wheel instead of timeless rubber tires. On the Plaza Tirso de Molina, a puppetshow begins at eleven o'clock, if the weather is good. The puppets, pronounced caricatures of good and evil, are, just like the Wayang shadow-puppets, moved by sticks on the hands and they rage at one another like Spanish furies. The puppet-show, incomprehensible to an outsider, is like a Dixieland Jazz number: the main lines of the story are fixed and around them is improvised. The show ends quite unexpectedly, exactly like a Dixieland number, but the moral of the story remains identical every time. At the end of the performance, an irresistible young girl goes around with the hat. It is an honor not to be permitted to miss the hat of this beauty. She also thinks so, even if she does look at things from a more concrete point of view.

From the Plaza de Tirso de Molina to the Plaza de Cascorro, where the 'Rastro' begins, is but a stone's throw. Just follow the crowds, like during the Carnaval in the south, but then a little differently: develop a sort of togetherness in order to fall apart into blissful individuality once the destination has been reached. Authentic Spanish!

In the sea of people, of which the tide only comes up at eleven o'clock, the small stalls stand indifferently in an apparently illogical order. Anyone may sell anything at the 'Rastro' and anyone may, with the permission of the neighborhood, open a stall. The only condition is that the vendor pay the symbolic fine of twenty-five pesetas (how many dimes did you say?) to a

*Watches, alarm-clocks, coins, necklaces
and ashtrays – pick and choose*

cheerful cop from the Madrid city authorities.
There are incredibly specialized stalls here. Take
for example the ones with flints, sun-glasses or
ceramic frog-families in all postures and sizes.
The most typical specialist is the seller of keys.
From him you can buy all sorts of keys: from the
stately key of an honorary citizen of Madrid to an
old-fashioned skeleton-key, in copper or bronze
and, made to order, in silver or gold.

The times have passed in which the well-to-do
inhabitants of Madrid would go to the 'Rastro'
after church to look for ornaments for their
homes. The dolled-up ladies of Madrid, looking
like stale cream-puffs from an old box, have
vanished from the streets. Probably the trade
was spoiled when the market in second-hand
clothes conquered the 'Rastro'. Not a single self-
respecting Spaniard wants to see his old clothes
again; neither in a heap nor on someone else. The
monied classes, which used to do something for
charity, have, as a result of their lack of comprehension of the shady distribution channels,
caused the demand for antiques to drop by stay-
ing away.

Of course they are there, the antique stalls
that is, where people are still proud of genuine
antiques and where they do not give a hoot for
the old trash from grandmother's day. On Ribera
de Curtidores, number twelve, there is a gallery
of small stores, where one realizes that profes-
sionalism can mean a masterpiece.
The gateway onto the patio invites you in for a
visit. On the left stands the unsellable statue of
Bacchus, who discovered that his neighbor, a
vestal virgin unrestrained by Freudian learning,
also liked fruit. Both are flanked by two negro
figures who have just missed the Olympic flame,
but this is made up for by the kneeling prelate
behind them who is still hoping that his prayers
will save what can be saved. All the statues are
so monstrous that they drive the visitors to the
small shops on the inner square.

With a bit of luck, you may be able to secure an
engraving from Amsterdam dating from 1589;
after all, the Spaniards of that time knew the
way in the Low Countries. Antique paintings by
famous artists are no rarity but considering the
art of bargaining, a knowledge of affairs is a
minimum requirement. At the entrance on the
right is a stairway, which is not scary. On the

first floor you have, besides an outstanding view
of the patio, a beautiful view on the other side of
the 'Rastro'. Across the roofs of the hundreds of
stalls, your eye falls immediately on the man
who is praising his polystyrene gliders made for
children. Together with his wife, he lets his articles flying during the entire Sunday above the
heads of his potential customers. He has been
doing this for years and for the time being this is
unlikely to change, because all kids love flying-
machines.

From the 'balcony of the Rastro', on the first
floor of the Galerias Nuevas, you have to return
to the ground floor. This can only be done by
turning left and walking past the little shop of
'Guillamon'. In this pleasant little place, hundreds of silver pocket-watches show the exact
same time every day. A similar type of gallery is
on the other side of the Ribera de Curtidores, at
number twenty-nine. The towers with their
archways to the inner quarters will not disap-
point you. On this patio, everything is grotesque:
lions sit waiting to guard the entrances to the
castles from the snooping public. On the first
floor – you can likewise choose between two
stately opera-like stairways – there are car-

riages from the Napoleonic Age and cribs from the French occupation, which are all waiting for their Francophile buyers. The crème de la crème of the antique world can be found a bit further on.

Galerias Ribera, at number fifteen, frightens one off at first with its noisy record store, which flings the top of the hit-parade over the flea market. The El Dorado for the antique lover is on the bottom floor, where no sounds from the market penetrate. The atmosphere is exquisite and not a single lady of Madrid would dare to walk around here unperfumed. Everything here is genuine, expensive and is delivered with a guarantee. Just like anywhere else, buying antiques is an art in itself. Getting them over the border is a tough proposition, for the export of antiques is prohibited by the law in Spain.

Madrid knows no Place du Tertre but a Calle de San Cayetano, where professional artists and amateurs can sell their goods. The dividing-line between the Sunday painter and the professional

artist is extremely fine: the amateurs are of such high caliber that you think that they could do even better. As far as that goes, the sellers leave a mistaken client to his error. The professional artists convey emotionality in their work through the simplicity of the material. The street-scenes, simply painted with a pallette knife in blacks and whites, are 'tipico' and arresting through their lack of complexity.

A little further on, also on the same side of the Ribera de Curtidores, you might think you were at the mini-birdmarket of Antwerp while you are actually in the Calle de Fray Ceferino Gonzáles. Here are all kinds of whistlers, amongst which are genuine chiff-chaffs, all with twenty-day guarantees provided you do not remove the rings from the legs. When making the purchase, make sure that the ring is firmly attached, otherwise the guarantee wil fly away of its own accord. You can talk for hours over a bird in a box or buy a shivering dog with a free photograph of its parents, 'Perritos de lujo', or a deluxe hound with a flea-free skin. 'Muy barato!' (Very cheap!).

Whatever the situation in the Middle-East, the Jews and the Arabs remain good friends at the 'Rastro'. Each of them has his own speciality. The Jews, somewhat more tradition-conscious than their Semitic brothers, keep to selling their own products: jewelry, Stars of David, and seven-armed candlestick-holders. The Arabs, mostly Moroccans, are specialized in leather-work and pornographic surprises: from pictures and films to small attractive boxes with colorful contents, which the aspiring, color-blind buyer overlooks. The gypsies at the 'Rastro' have the monopoly on watches, while their daughters dance and sing. The Chinese and Vietnamese sell their own hand-made pieces of work, which are put together with much patience and ingenuity.

De Plaza Del Campillo del Nuevo Mundo, 'the field of the new world', does honor to its name. On this little square, much intellectuality has gathered together. The biggest scene here is the dealing in second-hand magazines, enabling collectors to feast their eyes on the first editions of Flash Gordon. Once in a while, there is something in between that belongs more in a second-hand bookshop. Among the collectors of coins and medals, 'Captain Walter' sticks out head and shoulders above the rest. This German, who has been in Spain for more than twenty-five years, is doing the business of his life: he sells nostalgic souvenirs from the Third Reich and from the age of the Spanish dictatorship.

The 'Captain', a man of quite some years, wounded four times on the Russian front, looks lively with his battle-cap and army shirt. He is assisted with the selling by Spanish youths in black uniforms, who are, unlike their German chief, usually in a bad mood. 'Arriba España!; he says amiably, as he greets a Spanish friend with his right arm raised. 'Hola Camerada Walter', the other laughs, pleased at so much demonstration of recognition. Business is not bad: there are flags with glorious but abandoned inscriptions, Spanish-made 'Swastikas', medals and photographs.

'Captain Walter': 'The most photos that I sell are of Franco, followed by those of José Antonio Primo de Rivera, the founder of Spanish fascism, and only in the third place, photographs of Hitler... No, oddly enough I never did meet Hitler but I have seen Franco from close-by when I was received with a group in audience. A great man! There is no longer any ideological value behind the articles which I sell, *weisst Du. Ach ja, das leben ist in Spanien nicht so schlecht.* In Spain, I am not a member of any political party: as a foreigner you have to remain neutral, *nicht?* We sell all the badges in this field.'

'Captain Walter' feels very much at home at the 'Rastro'. 'Hola Camerada', says a Spanish enthusiast, *'Yo tambien soy fascista.'* (I am also a fascist). Completely different is the venerable Imam Karam Ilahi Zafar, who stands at his stall hardly twenty yards further on. This Mohamme-dan Hindu-leader mutters words from the Koran and in between sells water perfumed with jasmine and mixed with musk. He is a very serious person and is always prepared to assist anyone. No sinner is too bad for him. He is a man whom you do not forget quickly: if you shake his hand, two hours later you are still smelling of jasmine and musk. 'A message of Peace and a few words to consider', states the Imam with the best of intentions. *'Madre mía'*, thinks the Spaniard to himself as he buys a little bottle of scented water for his mother.

Second-hand clothes abound. From antique lace up to and including the old-fashioned, fine silk dresses from the time of grandmother's first communion. Holy Passion images by the score, and even the Spanish rendering of 'Here shall no one swear', are represented everywhere. There is religious art and kitsch aplenty, so much that you almost start to believe. The historical victory of the Spanish Catholics over the Moors has left its traces on the 'Rastro'. But actually, the Moors never had evil intentions. At the Ribera de Curtidores number thirty-three is a Moroccan store. Mohamed Touzain is patient, friendly and even speaks Dutch. Once a year he is off to his girl friend in Sneek, Holland and there he peps up quite a bit. On the corner of the Plaza del General Vara del Rey, where the streets Calle Mira el Rio Alta and the Calle de Carlos Arniches intersect, there is also an Arab store. None of the Arabs has a Dutch girlfriend though.

One thing will have probably disappeared if the 'Rastro' is still in existence in the future: 'El organillo', the Madrid street organ, that used to

Left: *Doves for the mantelpiece*

Below: *An incomprehensible mess for the uninitiated – paradise for the curiosity seeker*

Right: *Old cameras are mostly bought by collectors*

make the streets of Madrid ring with its crystal-clear sounds. There are sufficient organs but the organtuner is sick, the only man in the world who can tune them: his hands refuse to cooperate any longer. His last creation was the tuning of an organ for a record company which thereby immortalized his pure work. Because no one wants to buy an out of tune organ, they remain in the shops on the Plaza del General Vara del Rey getting dusty, with a brilliant 'Chotis' in their stomachs that hardly anyone will ever hear.

'Madrid...Madrid...' sounded the 'Chotis' once through the streets, which looked like colored rows of houses with winking windows. The old street-life of Madrid can still be brought inside by the primitive paintings on glass, typical Madrid folk-art, which was initiated by a now deceased German lady. The minatures are unique by virtue of their warm colors and their primitive style, which makes the faces of the people seem very close to you. Children in particular are attracted to these works. Of course, there is a lot of imitation among all this art: all the angry or motherly Madonnas are unpalatable. The city-scenes and the portrayals of children playing are palatable.

Rastrillo
The second flea market in Madrid is called the 'Rastrillo' and is held on Sundays from 9:00 to 15:00h, in the Calle Marqués de Viana. At the exit to the Valdeacederas subway, just mix with the crowds only to go your own way again at the 'Rastrillo'. This flea market is more a second-hand market for everyday articles of use than a gathering place for curiosities. The copper-work is completely in the hands of the gypsy women, who once in a while also dabble in textiles. Foreigners have hardly discovered this market but a single astute salesman has placed a sign in front of his stall with the English inscription: 'Yor sive terrier'. Not a single passer-by racks his brains trying to decipher this method of writing 'Terriers for sale'.

The postage-stamp exchange of Madrid, the largest in Europe, is unique. It is held every Sunday from 9:00 to 14:00h on the Plaza Mayor. There are two types of stamp-sellers: the legal dealers, who all have a small table at their disposal and the casuals, who have no fixed places.

For years the council of Madrid has been trying to get rid of these casuals but they defend themselves with the grandiose argument: 'If we disappear, then the postage-stamp exchange on the Plaza Mayor will no longer be the largest in Europe.' Collectors of coins, matches, cigarbands, and pictures of animals can do excellent business on the Plaza Mayor. The stamp exchange can be reached by various lines of the subway: exit Sol.

The book-stands of Madrid on the Calle de Claudio Moyano possess many secrets. You can find beautiful and valuable editions under the books on display but the racy books from the history of Spain still lie in the secret drawers of the stall. To ask for polemical books, most of which were forbidden during Franco's regime, is the same as striking up a deep and semi-intellectual friendship with all the book-sellers in the area. The book-sellers drop all feelings of competition towards one another for a customer who also wants to learn the other side of Spanish history. He becomes immediately their 'amigo' but this can only be achieved if you speak Spanish. The Madrid book-stalls are open every day from 9:00 to 14:00h and can be reached by subway: exit Atocha.

Selling is an art, buying a trade and vice versa. You have to have a feeling for it, especially in Spain, not just in order to con but to grant the joy of it to one another. It is a game, even though the Duke of Alva thought differently; but he could not help it: in his day there was no 'Rastro' yet and besides, the man was a poor loser.

Negotiating '*es un arte*'. Bargaining takes place discreetly and with a joke. Never let the public notice how well you can bargain and how much nerve you have for then the seller will make you look a fool. Do not walk away, as in an Arab country, because the Spaniard is proud. If you then come back, it is sooner a reason for the seller to raise the price, because he will know that you still do really want the object.

Create a climate of mutual trust which keeps the mean between comprehension of the asking price and a demonstration of the incapacity of the wallet. A good strategy, if there are two of you, is to share your money between you. Pretend during the purchase that you have to borrow money from your partner and he should then

Rastro Madrid

act a little hesitant in order to play the game well. Never bargain together, because then the seller will feel himself threatened by such superior odds and will clam up.

The best thing to do on hearing the price is to exclaim in alarm, 'Hombre!' Not too loudly of course, for then the Spanish public will take your side and the seller will clam up once again.

The seller will begin immediately with the praising of his goods and with the psychological manipulation of his customer. Calmly allow him to do so, thus respecting his professional honor. At the most say 'Pues', which you pronounce 'Pwes'. To look approving and to cough politely shows that you are considering. So far so good.

A fine move, especially for people with blond hair, who are immediately taken for foreigners, is the following sentence: '*És un precio turistico?*' In response to the question as to whether it is a tourist price – and therefore a higher one – the seller will lessen the distance between himself and the aspiring buyer. 'Of course not', the seller will then think, 'this customer is also one of us'. Just allow the seller to come on; a second 'Pues' at this point is quite appropriate.

If it concerns an antique and if the seller evidently has the time, then you can always take the initiative yourself by inviting the man for a cup of coffee. A third 'Pues' is not strictly necessary here but is certainly permissible. With '*Le*

**Barcelona
Plaza de las Glorias**

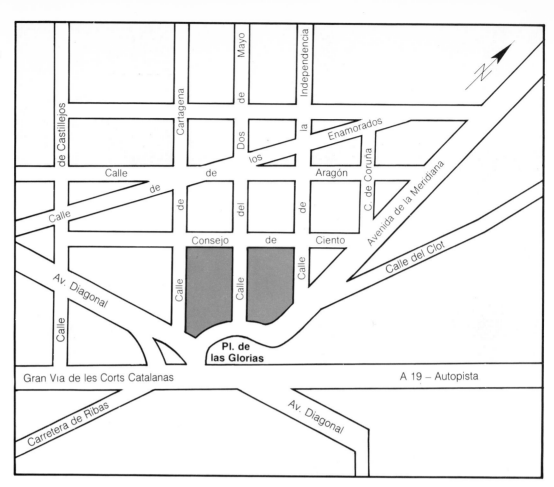

**Madrid
Rastro**

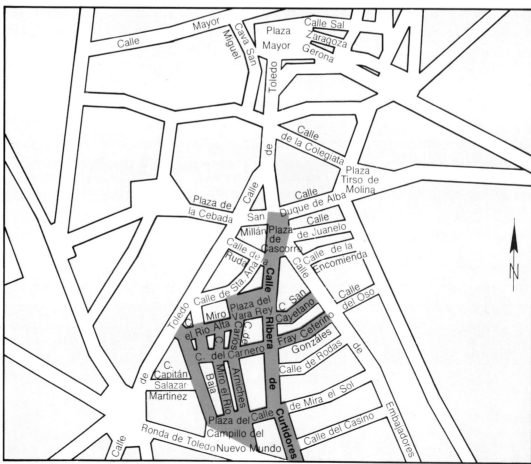

Flea markets Almería-Valladolid

Almería
● Mercadillo, in the suburb Regiones Devastadas, Tuesday from 8:00 to 14:00h

Barcelona
● Encantes San Antonio, c. Manso, c. Urgel, Monday Tuesday, Friday and Saturday from 9:00 to 21:00h
● Encantes Viejos or Feria de Bellcaire, c. Dos de Mayos, Plaza de las Glorias, daily from 7:00 to 19:00h

El Ferrol
● La Feria, Paseo de Mella, third Sunday of the month

Gerona
● Mercado of Mercadillo, c. Vayreda, in the months January to April and October to December from 9:00 to 13:00h
● Paseo de la Dehesa, in the months May to September from 9:00 to 13:00h

Gijón
● Rastro, Sunday

Ibiza
● Weekly Hippie Market in Punta Arabi (Es Cana): Monday
● Daily Hippie Market in the city Ibiza, c. Mayor: Also in the evenings
● Daily Hippie Market in the city San Antonio, opposite the night-club Sa Tanca, also in the evenings
● Daily Hippie Market beneath the city-gates of the old city Puerta de las Tablas. (All Hippie Markets are open only in the summer; the first three open only in the afternoon)

La Coruña
● Plaza de María Pita, Sunday from 11:00 to 14:00h

Madrid
● Rastro, Plaza Vara del Rey, c. del Carnero, Sunday from 9:00 to 14:00h, Monday through Saturday from 9:00 to 20:00h
● Rastrillo, c. Marques de Viana, Sunday from 9:00 to 15:00h

Marbella
● Antique market, Explanda de la Plaza de Toros, Andalucia La Nueva, Saturday morning

Palma de Mallorca
● Mercadillo, Plaza Instituto Balear, Saturday

Santander
● Boutique-Calé, La Plaza de la Esperanza, Monday morning and Thursday morning

Sevilla
● El Jueves, c. Feria, every Thursday

Valencia
● Small market on Sundays and public holidays, near the cathedral, specialized in the selling of azulejos and zocarats

Valladolid
● Mercado de Cantarranas, Plaza de Cantarranas, Sunday from 9:00 to 15:00h

invito a un café', the seller's heart will be touched and a mellow mood will be created. Make sure that you do the paying in the café, otherwise the seller will have the stronger position. Of course, he always does stand firmly in his shoes but he has to loosen up a little. In the final analysis, it is not the object that matters, for it can always be gotten rid of. For a Spaniard, it is of importance how he gets rid of something. Deep in his anti-capitalist heart, there is always room for a hearty chat, which he can keep as a precious memory. In their hearts, Spaniards do not give a damn about money, which is why they are such masters at spending it.

If you do not speak any Spanish, then you can proceed in the café by means of notes on which each puts his price. Do not write on these notes like a book-keeper or pass them on like a clerk would. With a little feeling for the bombastic and the dramatic, work on the imagination of the seller, interjecting once in a while another 'Pues'. A little brandy with the coffee can do wonders, for the client as well as the seller.

If the deal has been made, always, with some display of emotion, shake his hand and afterwards pat him on the back. This pat on the shoulder ought to be friendly and not too fatherly, because otherwise the seller will feel cheated, and he, as a proud Spaniard, will give you back your money immediately. It should be the same pat on the shoulder that you used to give to your fiancé when the crying-fit was over.

Thief Market Campo de Santa Clara: an oasis of peace in rushed Lisbon.
The client is king, even if he gets cheated

Portugal

'Mister thief, I am the poorest vendor of the market. Be kind to me because I have little children at home to support.' This plea hangs framed in one of the little stalls of Lisbon's flea market, 'Feira da Ladra' as the people of Lisbon would say: 'The Woman-Thief Market'. Behind the stand sits a full-blooded gypsy woman with pitch-black hair and eyes; in front of her, on the trestles, are her wares: old keys, a broken shower-hose, a primer-stove, a candlestick-holder, something looking like an ashtray and a clothes-iron from the year zero. No other scene typifies the 'thieves' market' more adequately.

But this scene is from years gone by. Like the goods, the name of the market has very little to do with the present. The origin lies somewhere in the eighteenth century: the flourishing of the nobility, wealth from Brazil and the misery of the plebs who made ends meet by smuggling and robbery. In the narrow streets of Lisbon, an eternal struggle blazed between corrupt cops and illegal street-hawkers, gypsies, foreigners and smugglers. Who the biggest rogues were, the royal guards or the outlaws, is now difficult to ascertain.

Only after the liberal revolution of 1820 which followed the withdrawal of the French troops who had been defeated at Waterloo under Napoleon, was a separate free-market established. Inside the plebs were allowed to carry on their semi-legal trade without fear of police persecution, only to be more succesfully dealt with outside. Today, one still finds in Lisbon, besides an army of beggars, a profusion of street-vendors. People with clotheshangers, band-aids or oranges, quite prepared to pay the fine but unappeasable if their goods are confiscated.

According to the Luso-Brazilian Encyclopoedia of 1966, 'feira da Ladra' is a corruption of 'feira do Lado', which means 'market on the side', that is, on the side of the Tagus, the place where the jumble-market used to be held. Even if this explanation does sound very scientific, it stinks of the Salarzaristic censorship which even the encyclopedia was not spared. As far as the censors were concerned, everything had to be clean and decent and the terms 'thieves' and 'pick-pockets' were nothing more than a 'people's wordgame'. And yet one will encounter little hinderance from pickpockets at the 'thieves' market'. This one will sooner find in the rushed, over-crowded subway, where one also encounters the fleas which suggest the English market-name.

The 'Campo de Santa Clara' where the 'thieves' market' is held, is an oasis of peace in the tumultuous capital. On the one side is the romantic Alfama, the characteristic sixteenth century suburb; on the other side, the Tagus, which once in a while can be seen through the market stalls like a fata morgana. It is cosy because of the mentality of the Portugese vendors who are always prepared to show everything, to discuss and to explain, and to wait patiently until the customer has made his choice. And even though a customer might never get so cheated in his life, he remains king. This applies in particular to the foreigners, those tourists for whom the 'thieves' market' has been a standard item on their itineraries for a long time. In their honor, it is not uncommon that prices are raised by a fat twenty percent. Not so surprising after all, because, as far as the Portuguese vendors are concerned, the rich tourists are simply part of the circle of customers of the less financially able people of Lisbon: people who want the commonplace as cheaply as possible. Especially outside the tourist season, the stalls with ready-made clothes and footwear dominate. Even furniture made of real plastic is for sale here, and further, there is other furniture, tools, radios and cassette recorders. Not just a jumble-market, it is more like a general trading-store: in the middle are the covered vegetable, fruit, fish and meat stands of the sort which one can find all over Portugal; more hygienic than the peasants' shops further on in the neighborhood, these are still in sharp contrast to what a North European or an American is used to at home.

The stalls with antiques, odds and ends and old rust (the distinction is not always made), can be found here and there scattered around the market. Some dealers possess a sturdy stall and display their wares neatly; others make do with a plastic floor-cloth and a square yard of side-walk. The more settled bric-à-brac-stalls ('brica-braque' in Portuguese) can be found above the gardens of the Military Court (on the corner of the Rua da Veronica). Even if what you are look-ing for is not on display, ask for it: you will be eagerly shown to the storageroom!

In the same corner, one can find the speciality of the Lisbon market: the old coin-exchange. Opposite that, if one looks carefully between the clothing-stalls, a stairway leads downwards to the convent of Santa Engrácia. Arranged neatly on both sides of the stairs, one can find the lesser gods of the bric-à-brac who are certainly a lot cheaper than their settled colleagues 'from above'. At any of these vendors, one can bump into a real surprise. In the poorest country in Europe, many things are being dumped as use-less and obsolete, which in wealthier areas bear the romantic memories of 'artless' and more 'genuine' times. But watch out: the old Christ-image with the broken arm is lying in abundance for sale in a stall further on with just as many broken arms. The 'Last Supper', entirely chased in zinc, framed and already turned green, is sold in another stall among Fatima-images, gypsy paintings and pink floor-lamps for much less: but then brandnew and... to the Portuguese!

The distinction between foreigners and fellow countrymen runs through the Lisbon market-happening like a red thread. Do not let this frighten you away, because the foreigner has an advantage over the simple Portuguese. That one over-worked and under-paid girl at the over-crowded camping-ground can be simply over-looked, though.

Less tourist-oriented are the various yearly markets spread throughout the country. The Portuguese are crazy about their 'feiras', often holding market and fair at the same time. These are always fun and always crowded. They some-times specialize in locally manufactured prod-ucts: earthenware, dinner-services, tapestry, rugs, wood-carvings and other handicrafts which are still being made in Portugal for everyday use. At these markets, one may also come across a fortune-seeker attempting to sell the most undefined of goods. Very famous is the 'Feira da Luz', held every year on the 27th of June, in the shadow of Lisbon's Benfica Stadium. It is a sort of super-jumble-market and fun-fair, where every flea market dealer from all over the dis-trict finds his place. Just like it is the 'Feira' of Cascais, held from the 15th to the 30th of July in the city-park of this tourist place. Here exists, of course, also the fondness of foreigners, who popu-late the 'gold coast' to the west of Lisbon in the peak seasons.

The real lover will be most is his element at the bi-weekly market of Sao Pedro da Sintra. This market is beautifully situated in one of Portugal's loveliest regions. The enthusiasm of the dealers and the quality of the proffered 'junk' allows this Sunday-market to compete outstand-ingly with the 'Feira da Ladra' in Lisbon. But also here one has to put up with the second-hand clothes and the shoes, the donkeys and the cick-ens, the pots and the pans, the fados (mournful Portuguese folk-songs) from cassette recorders and the aroma of freshly grilled sardines wafting from dingy diners.

Also Oporto, Portugal's second city in the far north, has its own jumble-market: the Feira de Vendôme. It is the only market in Portugal where exclusively jumble, bric-à-brac and sec-ond-hand goods are sold. The surface area is smaller than her big brother's in Lisbon but the supply is usually larger. This market is open to anyone wanting to get rid of something, which is why one often finds young people here wanting to palm off their books and records. The majority of the vendors, however, belong to a fixed group and they bemoan the fact that they do not have to pay for their sites. No permanent place is availa-ble to them and so they have to jostle early every Saturday morning for the best sites.

At the foot of the old, Romano-Gothic cathe-dral, situated high above the city, and in the narrow alley surrounding it, one can easily be-lieve himself to be in medieval times. And yet the atmosphere, for one reason or another, is less lively than in Lisbon. Perhaps this is as a result of the imposing church in the background or of

Lisbon
Feira da Ladra

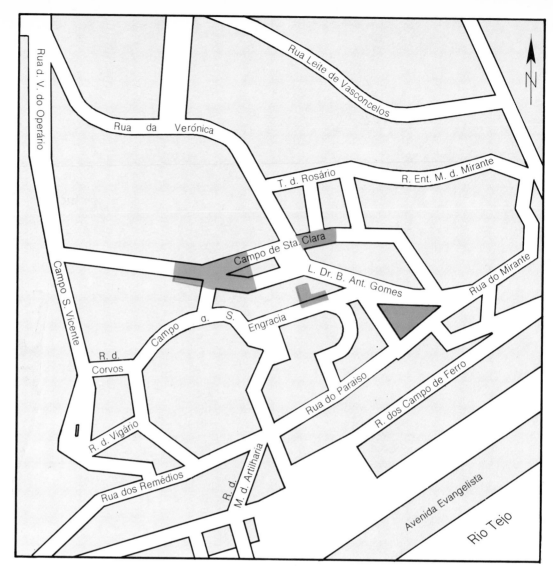

what the Portuguese call the dourness of their northern countrymen.

Completely different is the 'Feira da Ladra', which is held once a month in the parish-hall of the Cedofeita Church in Oporto. It is a charity sale which has been enjoying great interest for a good many years. The prices are low and the supply is often exceptionally good. Much has been donated by the parishers themselves. The opposite side to this coin is the not very appealing indoor surroundings in which the market is held. The real 'thieves' market' atmosphere is very far removed from these venerable citizens!

Flea markets Cascais-Sao Pedro da Sintra

Cascais
● Feira, city-park, 15th to 30th of July

Lisbon
● Feira da Ladra, Campo de Santa Clara, Tuesday and Saturday 10:00 to 18:00h
● Feira da Luz, near the Benfica Stadium, 27th of June
● Campo Santana, behind S. Vincente, Tuesday and Saturday

Oporto
● Feira da Ladra, in the bottom of the new Cedofeita Church, first Saturday and Sunday of the month from 10:00 to 13:00h and from 15:00 to 19:30h
● Feira de Vendôme, at the foot of the cathedral, Saturday

Sao Pedro da Sintra
● Feira da Sintra, second and fourth Sunday of the month

Rome's Altar-pieces are sweet,
19th century egg-shells from Milan,
but never forget Arezzo's 'fiera'!

Italy

Whoever has studied a random pamphlet or travel guide on Rome is immediately confronted with the many archeological treasures which the Italian capital has to offer in sometimes such overwhelming quantities. Whether it be the Vatican, the Citadel of Angels, the Spanish Steps or the Capitol, the Trevi Fountains or one of the elaborately decorated baroque churches, it all comes down to the past of this city which fascinates the visitor. In only a few instances is the attention focused on contempory attractions which are of special interest to the Italians and are over-looked by the average tourist.

To them belongs the large Sunday market, the beginning of which is situated close to the Porta Portese. Here the remains of the old city walls join up with the still remaining city gates situated on the south side of Trasteverre in the western part of Rome and beyond the Teverre, that is, the Tiber. Whatever other curious character-traits this remarkable Roman city may possess, it is not entitled only to boast about its miles-long market which begins just on the other side of the city wall – the Porta Portese will not be able to stimulate the average market-visitor for any length of time owing to its conspicuous lack of beauty.

Half past nine is a good starting time to take a walk through this market which, at its heart, possesses the goal of our interest: the flea market. By this time, the market has already been in progress for some one and a half hours, but this seems to be, for the multitude of Romans, far too early; the biggest rush occurs at about eleven o'clock, when church or family visiting is apparently over.

For our visit, the first part of the market is of lesser import. It covers the largest area of the Via Portense and consists of what at first seems to be a desolate piece of road. There are no houses, on both sides sheds have been put up or there are storage-places situated in niches under a street that runs parallel but which is situated higher up, the Clivo Portuense.

Most of the market-people who sell here come

Flea market in Arezzo on the first Sunday of the month

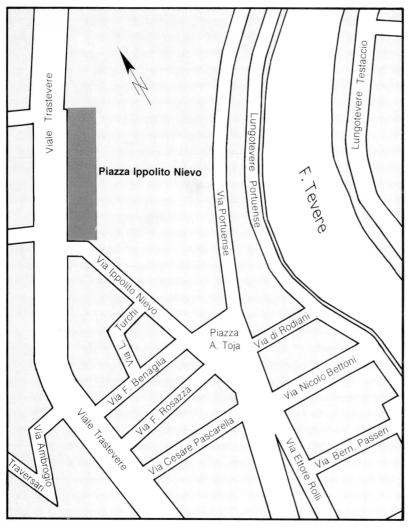

Rome
Porta Portese

from Rome or the immediate vicinity; only the odd dealer comes from much further away. Their supply of fur coats, leather, textiles and toys, all of it brand-new, stand in sharp contrast to the older articles which we have come for. These are for sale in the middle part of the market where the road forks. The actual marketplace runs out onto a small square, the Largo Allessandro Toja, which, at about eleven o'clock, already reveals a large crowd. It is the last two hours of the market, which will have ended by about one o'clock, but they are also the busiest, the most animated, after an otherwise uneventful early morning. The market stretches from the Largo Allessandro Toja to the Via Portuense, then goes into the Via Ettore and finally stops near the Via Pamfilo Castaldi. The actual flea market runs immediately from the small square, in the form of a side-branch, to the Piazza Ippolito Nievo, a square bordered by the boulevard-like Viale Trasteverre and a block of modern white houses.

Whoever compares the Roman flea market with what he has found in, for example, Amsterdam, Paris or Antwerp, will feel cheated in Rome. The character of the Roman market is not unpleasant even if it does strike most people how little the stall-holder does to praise his goods. He stands there somewhat quietly and there is no question of his shouting at the top of his lungs in order to sell his wares. Only in response to an emphatic request will he loosen himself from his resting-place and even then he has hardly anything to tell you about the goods he has for sale.

His wares are more or less antiques, with a stronger accent on the junk which, also in Italy, was mass-produced during the second half of the last century and the beginning of this one. The country, bearing the Holy See in its heart, must have had a fair number of concerns which applied themselves to the manufacturie of religious relics, those objects which have everything to do with the glorification and portrayal of Christ. In many of the stalls, his agonized eyes stare at you, competing for the most attention with the crucifix; here and there an altar-piece of dubious quality is also offered. Often made from porcelain or an ugly type of wood, most pieces, despite their clumsy expressions, are charming; but one has to like the insipid and sweet characters with which they are afflicted.

Flea markets Arezzo-Finalborgo

Arezzo (Toscana)
- Fiera Antiquaria, Piazza Grande, first Saturday and Sunday of the month

Arma di Taggia (Liguria)
- Fourth Saturday and Sunday of the month

Benevento (Campania)
- Piazza Risorgimento, Piazza Santa Maria, Wednesday and Saturday from 8:00 to 13:00h

Bologna (Emilia-Romagna)
- La Piazzola, Piazza 8 Agosto, Friday and Saturday from 7:00h until one hour before sunset

Casale Monferrato (Piemonte)
- Piazza Mazzini (Piazza del Cavallo), second Saturday and Sunday of the month from 7:00 to 20:00h

Catania (Sicilia)
- Piazza Carlo Alberto, Monday through Saturday from 8:00 to 13:00h

Cortona (Toscana)
- End of August until the end of September

Cosenza (Calabria)
- Via Lungo Crati De Seta, daily

Ferrara (Emilia-Romagna)
- Piazza Travaglio, Monday and Friday

Finalborgo (Liguria)
- 27th and 28th of March

The Christmas manger, religious paintings, a little shepherdess and many more sweet things compete for the buyer's favor

Italian paintings from the last century, which also have these sugary traits, must have been made for the commercial market, because this market in Rome is not the only place where they are offered in large quantities, sometimes not even cheaply. They are of pleasant landscape scenes in which the pine trees with their static postures dominate, or they are simply decorated with a few drowsy-looking cows in a wild mountain area, which must have had a direct link to the Biblical paradise. On the odd occasion, a reasonably painted canvas may be hanging, mainly at the beginning of the Piazza I. Nievo, where a well-stocked antiquarian usually stands. A genuine one, to be sure, who also has a

good supply of furniture for reasonable prices.

In Italy also, the oil-lamp has started on a long march to popularity but it is remarkable that these lamps at the Roman market are mainly all copies of lamps and must have been manufactured not so very long ago. The oil-lamp has existed in the form in which we know it today for less than a hundred years and many of them were made around the turn of the century, when electricity and gas had not yet been installed everywhere.

You may wonder whether a visit to the Roman market is worthwhile or not. Much will depend on what is in fashion at a given moment in a particular season and is therefore in supply. This

43

The 'Fiera di Senigallia' in Milan
Left: *Not only the paintings are reproductions*
Right: *Sunk in thought*
Below: *The wrought iron is not going too well today*
Below right: *Will he or will he not?*

45

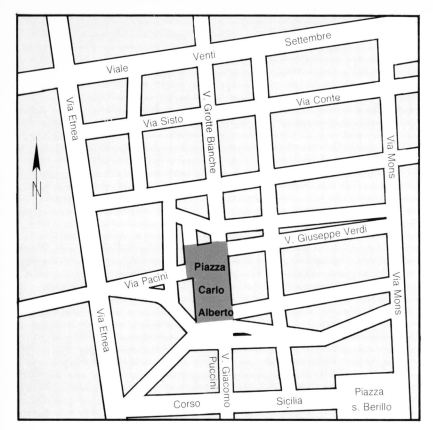

single antique may be present, which will not be worthwhile for everybody; but for that one collector who has long been looking for just such a piece, the visit will be amply compensated. Every flea market is a new adventure, an adventure that can vary from week to week. Rome has in addition to this market enough jumble-shops with better antiques which may offer just as much adventure.

Just as Rome is not the only important city in Italy, so the visitor to Italy need not limit himself to the Roman flea market. Whoever comes to this country for the markets will find enough in his or her line in other cities. For those who are interested, there now follows a brief summary of the other markets.

Piedmont

Turin offers a flea market every Saturday near the Porta Palazzo in the heart of the old city. This market is known to the inhabitants of this automobile-manufacturing city as Balón.

In Casale Monferrato, a market is held in the center of the city on the second Saturday and Sunday of every month on the Plazza Mazzini, known popularly as the Piazza del Cavallo.

Lombardy

Milan, for us the most important town in this area by far, sports two markets. A highly exceptional one is the Christmas market on the Piazza St. Ambrogio. Further, one is held every Saturday in the Via Calatafimi de Mercato di Senigallia. Here the most diverse of objects are displayed, from coach-lanterns and sewing-machines built in 1921 to egg-shells from the nineteenth century and clothes-irons which still operate on coal. Here the trade is lively, and exceptionally picturesque is the approach of some vendors, who, for example, offer products to fight insects or rheumatism to which the public are attracted by means of snakes.

Liguria

In Finalborgo (near Finale Ligure), a non-stop market is held in the medieval streets of the old city on the last Saturday and Sunday of the month. The city can be reached easily by train or with your own transportation. A bus runs from the train station to the center of the city. In Arma

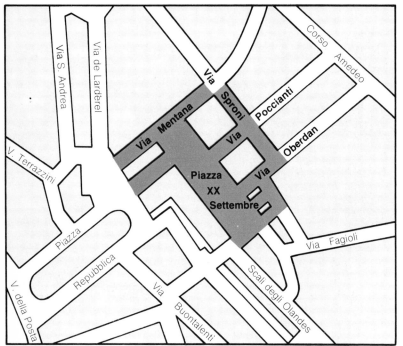

Livorno
Piazza XX
Settembre

is determined by the fluctuating taste of the public and, of course, by the people who go eagerly to the flea market to look around. The Roman market concentrates mainly on (phony) antiques, with the accent on domestic articles of mediocre quality. It is not a market at which one can expect numerous good bargains but this has become a general tendency of flea markets. A

46

di Taggia, there is also a market held on the last weekend of the month in the center of this historical city. It is an open-air market but offers protection against possible bad weather in the form of medieval galleries. This town can also be reached easily; there are city-buses.

Every workday there is a market held in Genoa on the Piazzetta Lavagna. In Genoa is also a so-called 'American market' with lots of dumpgoods which give the age-old streets a cheerful look. This market, called 'Shanghai' because of the many articles imported from the Far East, is situated in the city-center.

Emilia-Romagna
In Ferrara, a market is held twice a week: a busy one on Monday morning and a quieter one on Friday. Antiques and bric-à-brac penetrate onto the Piazza Travaglio, which is situated in the easily accessible city-center. Here too is a picturesque market in historical surroundings.

Bologna offers a market every Friday and Saturday with old and new on the Piazza VIII Agosto. The so-called 'La Piazzola' begins at seven o'clock in the morning.

Modena has a market every Monday morning but of more importance is the antique market which is held in this city on the fourth Saturday and Sunday of the month.

Tuscany
Livorno, it is true, has no flea market of its own but the 'Mercato Americano' on the Piazza XX Settembre, where the U.S. army dumps its surplus clothes, is certainly interesting.

Every Saturday and Sunday, a small market with antiques is held in Lucca. Arezzo has what may be the most important flea market in the whole of Italy. On the Fiera Antiquaria d'Arezzo, some six or seven hundred dealers arrive with the most diverse of goods. This market is held on the Piazza Grande, in the heart of the old city.

Florence has a number of markets at various times. Every day, except Sunday, one can visit a market at the Piazzo Ciompi, while in October, a first-class antique market is held in the Palazzo Strozzi. Naturally the prices here are not on a par with those of the average flea market but one can certainly go there for reasonably priced goods.

Flea markets Firence-Viareggio

Firenze (Florence) (Toscana)
- Piazza Ciompi, Monday through Saturday
- Palazzo Strozzi (antique market), October

Forte dei Marmi (Toscana)
- Piazza del Mercato, Wednesday morning

Genova (Genoa) (Liguria)
- Piazzetta Lavagna, Monday through Friday, mornings and afternoons
- 'Shanghai' (American Market), city-center

Grosseto (Toscana)
- Piazza De Maria, and below the walls, Thursday from 8:00 to 14:00h

Gubbio (Umbria)
- Via Baldassini (antique market), second Sunday of the month

Latina (Lazio)
- Mercato Americano, Via Quarto, Via Mugilla, Via Ardea, Via Sulmo, Tuesday from 8:00 to 13:30h

Livorno (Leghorn) (Toscana)
- Mercatino Americano, Piazza XX Septembre, Tuesday through Saturday from 9:00 to 19:30h

Lucca (Toscana)
- Piazza Duomo and surroundings, third Saturday and Sunday of the month, except on religious holidays

Messina (Sicilia)
- Via La Farina, corner of Viale Europa, every morning

Milano (Milan) (Lombardia)
- Fiera di Senigallia, Via Calatafimi, Saturday from 8:00 to 19:00h
- Fiera degli 'Oh bei! Oh bei!', Piazza S. Ambrogio, last Sunday of November; 6th, 7th and 8th of December

Modena (Emilia-Romagna)
- Via Caour, Viale Fontanelli-Berengario, Monday from 8:00 to 13:00h

Napoli (Naples) (Campania)
- Corso Malta, Poggioreale area, Monday and Friday
- Corso Novara, near the Central Station ('American Market')

Palermo (Sicilia)
- Piazza Domenico Peranni, daily from 9:00h to sunset; Sundays and holidays from 9:00 to 13:00h

Roma (Rome) (Lazio)
- Porta Portese, Sunday from 8:00 to 14:00h

Torino (Turin) (Piemonte)
- Il Balón, Porta Palazzo, Piazza della Republica, all day Saturday

Viareggio (Toscana)
- near the Darsena, Thursday morning

There are also markets in the following four cities: Forte dei Marmi, on the Piazza del Mercato, every Wednesday morning; Grosseto, on the Piazza de Maria, every Thursday, and in case of a holiday, the day before; Viareggio, near

Lovely articles at Arezzo's monthly antique market

Darsena, on every Thursday morning; and finally, Cortona, where an old furniture market is held from the end of August until the end of September.

Campania
Benevento has a market on the Piazza Risorgimento and on the Piazza S. Maria, every Wednesday and Saturday from 8:00 to 13:00h. Naples has two markets, one of which is a big American market near the train station in the Corso Novara. On Monday and Friday a market is held in the Corso Malta (in the Poggioreale area).

Calabria
Cosenza has a market every day in the Via Lungo Crati de Seta.

Sicily
Messina does not have a real flea market but does have an American market, also called 'Shanghai', opened on weekdays in the Corso Europa. Catania has a market on the Piazza Carlo Alberto, and Palermo has the Mercato delle Pulci (literally: flea market), on the Piazza Domenico Peranni.

Lazio
Latina has a pretty good-sized American market, which is held every Tuesday, except on holidays in the Gescal area in the Via Quarto and the Via Ardea.

Umbria
An antique market is held on the second Sunday of the month in the center of Gubbio.

48

Bargaining: an exhausting affair in Athens. The supply is abundant, especially of unimaginative mass-produced articles

Greece

The Greeks have managed to cut out just about all the influence on their daily lives of the long Turkish domination, but not from all the facets of their existence. Fortunately, one might say. So an almost authentic Eastern bustle and industriousness reigns at the flea market of Athens. In the alleys of the old city, around the Monastiraki Square, between the Ermou, Athinas and Eolou Streets, the tourists and the locals jostle one another in open shops, crowded stalls and stands, alongside fully loaded carts, travelling merchants, improvised eating-kitchens and in the dark workshops of the tradesmen. All the goods are displayed in such a manner that the curious customer is able to take in and compare the entire selection at a glance. The confusing profusion of curiosities presented in the extremely narrow space is perhaps the best way to directly inspire the inquisitive masses to buy. Strict order in drawers, compartments and cupboards has been banned from this branch of trade and small industry.

Advantageous for the visitor, and characteristic, is the situation of this old market. Approximately three hundred yards north of the Acropolis and close to the romantic suburb Plaka – the former Turkish area – the flea market borders directly on the antique market area of the Greek and Roman Agora. Even at the beginning of the nineteenth century, Athens must have been a city with an Oriental character in which the suburbs, in a typically stringent manner, were segregated according to class and population-group.

The supply of goods here does not differ essentially from that of a Turkish or Egyptian bazaar – in some areas it is clearly more oriented towards foreign buyers. Nevertheless, here too the broad range of genuine handcrafts, second-hand articles and mass-produced products lacking in fantasy is almost fully represented: ceramic jars, mostly with antique designs; carpets from Mykonos, Crete and northern Greece; kelims, colored woven products from sheep's wool, cotton and silk; tagarias, the carry-bags of all shapes and sizes which are so loved by both locals and tourists alike; woolen blankets and cheerfully embroidered slippers. The supply of red and green copper objects is the most oriented towards the Oriental examples without actually being able to compete seriously with them, either as far as the wealth of forms and decorations go or in quality and price. The ornaments consist time and again of antique patterns and motifs in all kinds of variations, geometrical figures, more or less stylized elements from the Mediterranean

flora and fauna, flowers, fish, birds, dolphins and snakes. Besides these, one can discover decorations influenced by Byzantine and Oriental designs over and over again.

Purchasing antiques can be a risky undertaking for the layman in every way. But the big demand for such objects was reason enough for a few Athenian museums to have accurate copies manufactured of famous pieces, which were then put on sale at reasonable prices. To this end, the Benaki Museum 'applied' itself to the reproduction of antique jewelry, while the National Archeological Museum offers copies of antique ceramics.

The supply of goods at the Athens flea market is certainly not restricted to art products; an even bigger share is taken up by everyday articles of use. Whether or not the recommended goods are still used for the purpose for which they were made is indeed questionable. Some dealers have applied themselves to selling old machine spare parts, household articles, scales, tools and rusty bicycle and automobile accessories. In dark, indoor places, but also in the middle of the alley, the tradesmen carry on their repair work or occupy themselves with manufacturing new objects. Tailors, carpenters, shoemakers, tinsmiths, blacksmiths, tinkers, woodworkers, furriers...

Nestling everywhere among these stalls and tradesmen are the stands and stalls of dealers who take care of the physical well-being of the market-visitors with their candy, drinks, grilled meat and other delicacies, because trading and

49

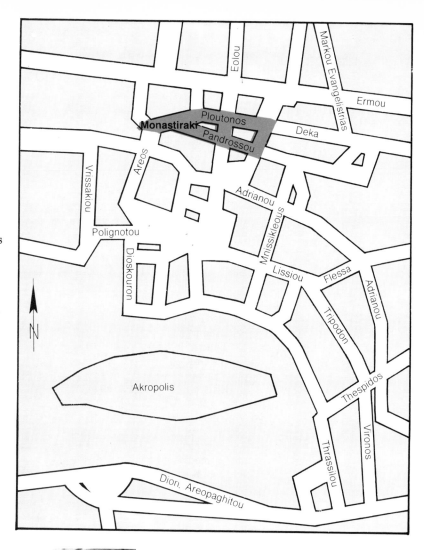

bargaining is an exhausting business, making, as it does, demands on all the senses.

In the narrow Pandrous Street, the Athens flea market is at its most colorful. Antique shops offer a survey of nearly all the periods of Greece's art history, usually having amazingly accurate imitations or forgeries of coins, small pieces of sculpture in bronze, clay or stone, sometimes also new casts from old moulds, paintings, icons and religious articles. Such sacral objects accompany the Greek in all areas of his life as an almost obligatory ingredient, at home, in the automobile and at work. More than other southerners, the Greek has a more naïve, imperturbable relationship to these religious objects, which are, however, very seldom to our taste.

Much could still be said about weapons, discarded medals, furniture, old cameras, gramophones, worn-out clothing, yellowed notebooks, pictures and also about the vegetable and herb stalls a few paces further on. The old market of Athens encompasses much in itself: it is a flea market as well as a bazaar, annual fair, trade and shopping center, place of small industry and, finally, also a bit of an amusement area.

Athens
Monastiraki Square

Flea market Athens

Athens
- Monastiraki Square and vicinity, Saturday and Sunday morning

Domino players on one of the many terraces around the market

Lucky finds at the Fetzenmarkt
in Graz. Reminders of the
Biedermeier Age. A freak in Vienna

Austria

The so-called 'Fetzenmarkt' (literally: rag market), that since the time of Empress Maria Theresia has been held four times a year in Graz, is still now a fruitful finding-place for all sorts of collectors. Not so long ago, the continued existence of this market was endangered. Karl von Holtei, Eugen Roth, Max Mell and many other important personalities have written about this famous market. The recently deceased Professor Paul Anton Keller of Graz participated in the struggle to keep the market going and about this, but especially about its history, told the following:

'Letters also have a destiny, particularly when one sends them to the newspapers. So it was with me after I had let some 'submitted letters' be printed in a Graz newspaper. They had as theme the complaint that people wanted to deprive the so-called 'Fetzenmarkt' of its existence, 'to get rid of it bloodlessly', and that it had therefore been transferred to an impractical square which the people, buyers as well as the vendors, would never accept. And so it was that I received an enormous amount of mail at home from persons who all absolutely agreed with me (not to mention two negative reactions to which I shall return, as I had much amusement from them). I then pointed out in a third letter that it was risky to choose such a square as had then been chosen, surrounded as it was by streets through which the busiest traffic of the city rages, and that it would be dangerous for those people who come to sell things, mostly elderly people who transport their goods with some difficulty by means of hand-carts. The letter was not published.

'And then a pretty young lady came to me and wanted me to tell her about the beloved market, for she had heard that I, indeed not in terms of age but in terms of 'market-visitor-age', was one of the oldest. That figures, because since my childhood, for about sixty years therefore, I have visited the 'Fetzenmarkt', and, as far as purchases go, never without success, (that is, with much finder's luck). She had also heard that I knew a lot about the history of the market of this city and that I intended in due course to publish a book, a kind of anthology, on the 'Fetzenmarkt' of Graz.

'Of course', I said, 'the Fetzenmarkt of Graz has a history; one that even goes back a long way; it is absolutely beyond me why people should want to liquidate such a beloved affair, which has become a general folk-festivity. And this at a time in which around us in Europe the

'flea markets' are all coming into existence; in London, for example, the famous 'Petticoat Market' is held every Sunday throughout the year and it is a lot more turbulent than at the market in Graz. And all these markets have been transferred to the liveliest and most densely populated streets.'

'Complaints have also reached our editors expressing displeasure whit those who want to have the market moved. Do you have any idea as to why they would want the market moved?'

'An idea I do have, but what use is that? Undoubtedly the motorists are getting all steamed up at the fact that their parking-places on the edge of the Augarten – for which they do not have to pay – are unavailable for two days. The house-owners, too, maybe because they have to keep their gates locked for reasons of security. But in 1959, the then mayor of Graz pointed out in a letter which he had submitted that the Fetzenmarkt has a social value, and that about four hundred vendors and approximately five hundred private sellers make use of the market regularly. Market rights were granted to the people in the middle ages and, in 1749, solemnly ratified by Empress Maria Theresia. The mayor stated further that the market can only survive in a place where people come together. If someone wants either to move the annual market of Graz or to ban it, then first the two Houses of Parliament will have to determine their own standpoint on the question; but these have repeatedly protested against such procedures.'

'Nevertheless, the market has now been transferred to a site that is utterly impractical for the use for which it is intended. Do they want it to pine away and die there?'

'That 'pining away', if you want to put it like that, is at any rate clearly observable and underground, something of a 'tug-of-war', a 'wrestling' can still be noticed. At the last market people offered the vendors beer in exchange for their signatures if they agreed that the market remain where it now is. When I asked a vendor, who had indignantly rejected the proposition, for his opinion, he replied with a melancholy face that he was ill with home-sickness for the 'old trusted Fetzenmarkt Square'. It was a strange effusion that I could really understand.'

Do you have an explanation for this hanging on to the old and trusted?'

'But of course! I have already told you that the 'Fetzenmarkt' is a sort of folk-festival which the people in the city and from the countryside look forward to with much pleasure. People should not always look upon folk-festivals in the spirit of folklore doings with jigging and similar bally-

hoo. The 'Fetzenmarkt of Graz' has a very special character of its own which goes back centuries. You can imagine that I could write a whole book of anecdotes were I to note down everything I have experienced there. In the first place, 'Fetzenmarkt', a name dating back to the Biedermeier Age (1815-1848), is only a collective name for four markets: Mid-Lent market in March; Portiuncula market (Patschungerl market) on the first of August; the Aegidius market on the first of September; and finally, the Andreus market in December. The markets in this form crystallized out of the ancient market-happenings of Graz; they are, in a manner of speaking, an offshoot of the two big annual fairs, which always lasted fourteen days, and which can look back on a history of some eight hundred years. The famous lexicographer, Heinrich Zedler, reported in 1735 on the 'two important markets or fairs at Mid-Lent and St. Aegidius'. At that time, the 'Fetzenmarkts' were an accompanying phenomenon of the big markets – J.B. Hofrichter from Graz writes in 1855 in his 'Rückblicken' about the 'remarkable jumble-markets (generally called the Fetzenmarkt)'. Finally, the market-freedom of Graz concentrated itself on two big markets in the spring, and on the small offshoot Fetzenmarkt in the fall.'

'Why the name 'Fetzenmarkt' then?'

'That is a trivial word coming from the old days; it is misleading, it is true, but is has become a popular concept. Just imagine, the poet-playwright, Carl von Holtei, who has almost been forgotten now wrote in his memoirs: 'If Graz would have nothing but the Schlossberg and the 'Fetzenmarkt', then this would still be enough to bind me to her!' One should not make the mistake of thinking that these annual folk-markets were only a gathering place of 'Fetzen' or rags!'

'Whoever leafs through the first volume of Peter Rosegger's 'Heimgarten' (1871), will find there a wonderful reminiscence of his first visit to the 'Fetzenmarkt' (and we shall therefore stick to the term 'Fetzenmarkt'). At about this time, the important water-color painter, Johann Passini (1798-1874), did a painting of this market, just as the painter Martha Fossel from Graz was to do many decades later.

'When I, as already mentioned, became a mar-

Vienna
Am Naschmarkt

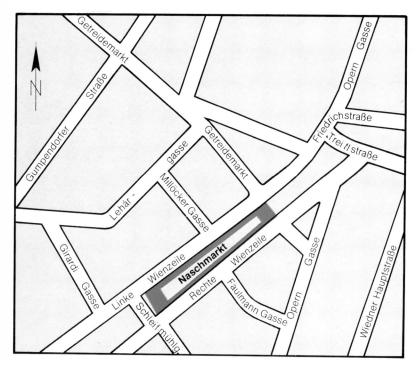

Flea markets Graz-Vienna

Graz
● Fetzenmarkt, four times a year for two days: in March, August, September and November.

Vienna
● Platz am Hof, Saturday from 9:00 to 17:00h
● Am Naschmarkt, Saturday from 8:00 to 19:00h

*Grubbing about in
the old clothes at the
'Fetzenmarkt' in
Graz*

ket-visitor more than a half a century ago – since then I have missed only one through illness – the stalls and stands encompassed the Flosslendplatz, Lendplatz and Volksgarten. The bookstore Cieslar often got rid of its stocks there and the unforgetable Rudolf Fischer, a fantastic bookdealer, the likes of which no longer exist, sold me, from the Cieslar stand next to the Andräkirche, a four-part Rosegger edition on semiparchment. This market near the Andräkirche, where in olden times mainly textile dealers offered their goods for sale, was already mentioned in charters in 1514.

'One should bear in mind that Graz, as the 'pensionopolis' of the old nobility and retired generals, could boast of many private art collections. Owing to a series of coincidences, it came about that the caretakers carted off valuables from such estates to the market without knowing exactly what they were putting up for sale. Antonie von Kaiserfeld writes in her 'Erinnerungen einer Fünfundachtzigjährigen' (1932) that her father had obtained, at the 'so-called Fetzenmarkt in Graz', a large altar-piece of Paolo Veronese. The painting was in terrible condition but it was later restored and is now in the possession of the Vienna council. Anticipating the history, I will tell you of the fortunate find that was made a few years ago – unfortunately not by me – at the market. During the Mid-Lent market, a little old lady had some pans, an umbrella and a cracked painting on display. A marketvisitor, Dr. H., bought the canvas. It looked awful. At home he washed it and sat admiring the lovely portrait of a woman which had emerged, although naturally the fell hand of time had left its murderous traces behind. To cut a long story short: it was an original work by Annibale Carracci from the sixteenth century. An art dealer offered right off ten thousand marks for it! And in the thirties, the old antique dealer Eisenstädter confessed to me that he had made the deal of his life at the 'Fetzenmarkt'. It was on a cloudy Portiuncula day and he was on his way home from the market when he saw how an old man, who had a cart full of old iron, was covering this conglomeration with a large cover. Eisenstädter recognizes it immediately as being an authentic Flemish wall-carpet. He bought it and, because the old man did not

wish to expose his old iron to the rain, he promptly bought all of that as well.

'Robert Hammlering was also a faithful market-visitor who knew exactly how to bargain and he brought many wonderful things home with him from the market. And Eugen Roth, the 'Ein Mensch – Roth', a famous collector, writes in his book 'Sammelsurium' about the market of Graz which he had visited, and so did Annie Francé-Harrar, wife of the renowned biologist and herself a scientist of some repute, in her memories 'So war's um 1900'. Forty years ago, the arctic-explorer Dr. Felix König travelled with a large group from Greenland to Graz, his birthplace, only on account of the two Andreus markets! Max Mell, in one of his most beautiful novels, 'Hans Hochgedacht und sein Weib', has a large part of the action take place at the 'Fetzenmarkt' of Graz. There is also a wonderfully recounted recollection by Walter H. Kotas (pseudonym Clemens Berg), in which he tells how he, as a young child – without money – was leafing longingly through two volumes of the magazine 'Jugend'. An old gentleman next to him asked: 'Would you like very much to have those books?' Kotas nodded. 'Yes, but I don't have enough money.' 'Well then, just take them,' said the old gentleman who then paid. When he had gone, the salesgirl asked: 'Do you know who that gentleman is? The poet Rosegger!'

'But one ought not to think that such lucky finds at the 'Fetzenmarkt' are not longer possible. Those who search intelligently can still reap a rich harvest.

'I have already said that I have been a visitor to the market for more than half a century. What treasures did the old Mrs. Bors have, standing-place Netzgasse am Murkai, which she let go dirt cheap, genuine minatures and Biedermeier glasses included! Her son, himself 'getting on in years', follows the tradition by still standing for a couple of hours at the market – without antiques, it is true – but if we meet each other, then we dream about the 'Fetzenmarkt' as it once used to be. For many years Max Mell and I went there together, which is to say, on the grounds of the market our paths diverged, because nothing is more cumbersome than a guide. But halfway through the morning, we would meet each other at the Augarten and that hour was dedicated to

books and reminiscing. Victor von Geramb was often on his way as soon as the market began. He once bought, from right under my nose, the entire collected works of Caroline Pichler in beautiful Biedermeier parts. I am still angry with him. I myself once found a series of lovely watercolors by Ernst Christian Moser (which a woman official from a museum later coaxed me out of); wonderful first editions of classical authors; Rosegger-tapes, with hand-written directions from the poet; a large file from the estate of Wilhelm von Tegetthof – hell, I guess that if I were to mention all the finds which others and myself have made, it would fill pages!

'An old woman vendor, who saw my briefcase full of books, began praising a book that was 'so lovely to read'. It was a work of my own, 'Sausaler Jahr'. I had already given all my presentation copies away, so I bought it; now I have my own book once again.

'When the 'Fetzenmarkt' was in danger, I wrote admonishingly to the newspapers. I felt that I had do so as a token of my appreciation for the innumerable happy days spent there. As I have already mentioned, besides the many letters, I also received an anonymous telephone-call, a real cannon-blast of abuse. I managed to trace the number, and, pleased as punch, reported it to the press. If that unsuccessful anonymity now sees me, he walks past me with a cowed look. In the only poison-pen letter which I received, obviously with no return address, someone else wrote: 'If the 'Fetzenmarkt' means so much to you then you should let it be held on your own premises!' That was a good one! It is really wonderful to know that there are asses around and that once in a while one hears them bray'.

So much for Professor Keller on the 'Fetzenmarkt' of Graz, which, for collectors and lovers of flea markets, is still very much worth the trip.

In contrast to this market, the largest modern flea market in Austria which since a few years ago can be found in Vienna, is very young. Originally it was held on the square am Alten Hof in the city-center. That became too small and it was necessary to move onto the larger 'Naschmarkt'. This long rectangular square takes its name from the big fruit and food market which, after the river Vienna was covered at the turn of the

*Leo Heusinger, chairman of the Vienna
flea market, is a conspicuous presence*

A permanent attribute of the Vienna flea market vendor is the high hat

century, used to take place and which was called the 'Naschmarkt' (literally: candy market). At the present, this huge market has been moved to the outer suburb Inzerdorf.

In the summer, a flea market is organized every Saturday from 8:00 to 20:00h by the Vienna Flea Market Association, which has as its chairman Leo Heusinger, a genuine Viennese freak. In wild colorful clothing, always cheer-fully engaged in conversation with prominent or less prominent visitors, one can come across him amidst the weekly teeming masses. Young and old, rich and poor, laborers, housewives, ministers, actors and conductors all nose around enthusiastically in the stalls; and hardly any of them know that, under the paving on which they are standing, the Vienna, covered at the turn of the century, once flowed on towards the Danube.

Switzerland's largest fleamarket festivity: brocanteurs in idyllic Le Landeron maintain the old city-center

Switzerland

The most well-known flea markets of Switzerland are held regularly every Saturday: in Basel, in the Münsterplatz high above the Rhine; in Zurich, from May to September, on the Bürkliplatz on the bank of the lake; in Locarno, Vevey and Lugano; and in Geneva, on the broad rhombus of the Plaine de Plainpalais, the market is held moreover every Wednesday. Anyone is permitted to set up a stall provided a permit has been applied for in advance and it is then always generously granted by the City of Geneva. The colorful supply of goods here varies from baby-pacifiers, irons, pans, cheap novels and cameras to four-poster beds.

The youngest and most romantic flea market in Switzerland had been in existence only since 1974. In that year, in the charming mediaeval town of Le Landeron, situated on the south-west edge of the Bieler Lake in a French-speaking area, a 'Fête de la brocante' was organized, 'the biggest junk-market festival in Switzerland'.

'Brocante' is strictly speaking a concept which is unknown to the Swiss. Actually, it is quite simply a name for the trade in second-hand goods but characterizes a level which is not represented by either the avowed dealers and ragmen, or by the actual art and antique dealers. 'Brocanteurs' are those dealers who offer the type of second-hand goods for sale at flea markets which are not utter trash but which may consist of very high quality, valuable antiques and works of art. They trade in the antiques of the 'middle classes', as it is nowadays termed in the German advertisements. Maybe we should also call them, in distinction to their more pretentious as well as their more modest colleagues, quite simply 'brocanteurs', as people have been doing for a long time in Switzerland.

These 'brocanteurs' dominate the appearance of the streets in Le Landeron, or more precisely, the idyllic, tree-shadowed rectangle between the old rows of houses of the city whose rear sides originally formed simultaneously the city-wall. Once a year, at the end of September, this unique antique festival, which has already become a tradition, is held. Visitors from Switzerland and neighboring France and Germany stream by the thousands to the picturesque town on the Bieler Lake. For two days, from Saturday through Sunday, the festival takes place beginning at eight o'clock in the morning and ending at seven o'clock in the evening.

More than a hundred and fifty vendors and antique dealers from all over Switzerland and the principality of Lichtenstein enliven the historical city-center and entrance roads with an indescribable confusion of wares.

Piled up, hanging and spread out, the objects are presented to the expectant public: beautiful cupboards, elaborately decorated chests of drawers, old engravings, dinner services, wax and porcelain dolls, articles of copper or tin, jewelry and clothing. Rarities lie next to less singular objects, while erotic picture-postcards await alongside the *oeuvre* of a famous master for new admirers. Old toys gladden the younger generations and bring back memories to the minds of the older visitors. And on one of the corners, the well-known actor, René Quellet, sells copies from his enormous collection of old jazz records.

A barrel-organ plays unforgettable melodies, while another one attracts a group of listeners with its sweet sounds. Here there is bargaining going on while further on people are nosing around. Greetings, tips or jokes are shouted about and goods which have been sold are carried away and replaced by others. At both of the town's restored wells, wine produced in the district is served, and many a thirst is quenched.

The old castle square is covered and has been converted into a festive restaurant. A dozen waitresses bring grilled cocks, fish and sausages,

The weather and the customers provide the vendors in Zurich with little reason for satisfaction ▶

58

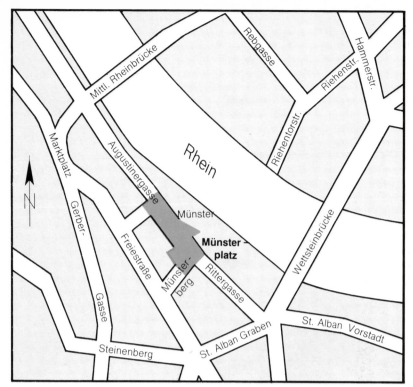

Basel
Münsterplatz

and one has the feeling that one has been placed back in a complete medieval happening.

Beyond the gates of the city, the industriousness continues. Here also one finds antiques, with artisans and their self-manufactured products, such as leather-goods, bags, belts, baskets, woven and knitted articles, earthenware, candles and jewelry, in amongst them. On Saturday, the usual weekly market is held with fruit, vegetables, eggs, flowers, fish, cheese, bread and pastries. The stalls of this market are set up outside the city-gates because the traditional standing-place on the large rectangular square

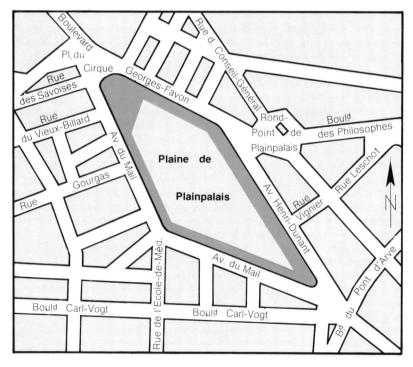

Geneva
Plaine de
Plainpalais

Left: *Colorful furniture on the Plaine de Plainpalais in Geneva*

Right: *This beautiful roundabout horse in Basel has undoubtedly had to make way for a plastic specimen*

within the gates has, for this one time, been left to the 'brocantes'.

In this respect, people in Le Landeron are very unselfish. The by no means negligible profit made at Switzerland's biggest flea market flows into a fund for the preservation of the old city-center and thereby for the preservation of the pretty surroundings in which it is held.

Flea markets Basel-Zurich

Basel
• Münsterplatz, Saturday from 9:00 to 16:00h

Geneva
• La Plaine de Plainpalais, Wednesday and Saturday from 8:00 to 17:00h

Le Landeron
• The old city-center, once a year: end of September

Locarno
• City-center, from mid-April, every second week

Lugano
• Via Nasse, Saturday afternoon, from May to mid-October

Vevey
• Place du Marché, Saturday, from 10th of July to 4th of September

Zurich
• Bürkliplatz, Saturday from 9:00 to 16:00h, from May until the end of October

The flea market festival in Le Landeron takes place amidst a wonderful medieval setting

62

Fill your bottle with a liquid which increases potency
Hang out in a dress-suit and evening gown near Altona
The longing for a discarded locomotive

West Germany

In West Germany, regular flea markets can be found not only in Munich, Hamburg, Stuttgart and Nuremberg, but also in a host of other cities. They are organized by the city authorities and every dealer or private individual can hire a stand and participate as vendor. These markets take place only on Saturdays, throughout the year: for example, in Göttingen by the old brickyard in the area of the Otto-Frey-Brücke and in the old city-center of Hanover on the Leibniz-Ufer. In the old Royal Park of Bonn, a flea market is held from May to September, but then only on the first Saturday of the month; in Munster, one is held from May to October on the Servatii-Promenade, also on the first Saturday of the month; and from April to December, there is one on the Schlossplatz in Oldenburg. On the other hand, throughout the year in Mainz, a public flea market is held on every second Saturday of the month on the Rathausplatz.

The supply of goods is everywhere just as diverse and plentiful and is also, from case to case, just as surprising as that found in Frankfurt, for example, or in Munich or on the Elbe in Hamburg. The advantage of these recurring weekly or monthly markets held on the same premises is that the collectors especially can gear themselves for them. One often comes across the same groups of people at the same places who are out buying, selling or swapping records, cheap paperbacks, postcards, dolls, old tin toys and a thousand and one other items, which are always indeed critically appraised at their exact cash value for the lover but which change hands just as often by means of an exchange.

There are now in Germany, besides the markets organized by the councils, also a series of commercial, in a manner of speaking, ambulatory market enterprises, which travel more or less regularly every weekend from city to city, mostly holding a market somewhere different on Sunday than on Saturday; these provide all the respective regions with odds and ends, old goods, rarities, curiosities and sometimes valuable antiques. They apparently seldom get in each other's way and have more or less marked out their territories amongst themselves. Their flea markets take place only on Saturday or Sunday and are sometimes also called junk-markets, second-hand markets, collectors exchanges or rarity-and-curiosity exchanges.

One of the most important of these enterprises is the market company 'Jadzejeweski' from Iserlohn which, covers the Lower Rhine to the Sauerland and into Lippe and Westfalen and 'serves' places like Recklinghausen, Wesel, Bochum, Detmold, Lüdenscheid, Brilon, Hamm, Iserlohn, Soest, Bocholt and Neuss. These places are visited about every sixth to eighth week. Duisburg, Münster, Dortmund and Ottermarsbocholt are, on the other hand, supplied by Rudi Pressel from Ascheberg. The Intax-Exhibitions-Limited, from the Zwabic Rottenberg, operates in Nuremberg, Augsburg, Mainz and Ulm amongst other places. The firm Klaus Krecky, from Herford, is in turn active in the district ranging from the Lower Rhine up to the North and East Sea, without colliding with its associates from Iserlohn or Ascheberg. This firm organizes flea markets regularly in Cloppenburg, Herford, Fulda, Goslar, Bremerhaven, Wolfsburg, Lübeck, Rade, Herne, Stadthagen, Rheine, Warendorf, Vechta, Uelzen, Mönchengladbach, Hildesheim, Nordheim and Nienburg on the Weser. In the south-west of Germany, travelling flea market organizer Hans Wehr from Worms regularly sees to markets in Neustadt, Bad Kreuznach, Frankenthal, Worms, Weinheim, Happenheim and Ludwigshafen.

The so-called 'Rode Enterprise Firm' from Katlenburg am Harz occupies, in a certain sense, an extraordinary position among travelling market organizers. This concerns not only the duration of the markets, which, under Hans Wehr's supervision, are open at least from Friday through Sunday in the larger cities and which are held in hired halls, but also the quality of the goods he has on offer. These are often more than just the old stoff which one generally finds at other junk markets. The attempt of this firm to

Bad weather? No problem. Just dress warmly, and everything can continue

Buying your assembly kit at a travelling flea market (here in Bremerhaven) can make quite a difference to your pocket-money

give its markets the pretentious name of 'antique exchange' and to set up a so-called overall organization of the German art and antique trade came in for heavy fire from the serious German antique dealers, who are organized in the traditional German Association of Art and Antique Dealers. Rode had to back out of the apparently exaggerated recomendation of its markets and its intended organization. In fact, it appears that Rode wished to establish something which, unlike in France, does not occur in Germanic countries: the so-called 'brocante', a kind of in-between level of the art and antique trade, which neither strives for the high standards (and prices) of the traditional art and antiques trade nor deals with exclusively second-hand goods and discarded household articles. In any event, the firm Rode attempts to offer more antiques than old goods at its markets but also those who nose around eagerly for a good find can enjoy themselves to their heart's content, just like at any other flea market or antique exchange.

At this point, the following comment is probably a propos: although the word 'antique' means nothing more than simply 'old goods' or 'used articles', the antique dealer therefore – according to the strict meaning of the word – is just as much a dealer in second-hand wares as the ragman of the street is. But a far higher value is attributed to an antique object, according to everyday language as well as to the trade rights, than to all normal second-hand goods. 'Antique', also in the formulation of the German customs restrictions, is something different from, and more valuable than, the mass junk of the flea markets and should therefore enjoy a certain protection by dint of the name, not in the last instance to the advantage of the collector and flea market fan. This is so that unexperienced and trusting hobbyists, who are themselves not capable of passing expert judgements and who are thus reliant on the advice of the seller, could not be deceived by the pretentious concept 'antique', when it concerns nothing more than an inferior object to which the attributes named by the dealer, such as age, style, material, origin and quality, definitely do not apply.

Someone who has a stall at a flea market can seldom quarantee any claims on this score because he does not possess the necessary knowledge himself. If this type of information is provided by an art or antique dealer who is a member of the German professional association, then this not so easily come by. Membership guarantees a certain amount of expert knowledge. As a dealer registered at the Chamber of Commerce, he must and will reimburse a client completely should he, which can happen to anyone, be mistaken in his statements. According to the German law, he is fully responsible until six months after the purchase. Many antique dealers voluntarily give their clients a longer guarantee on request.

One does not have this security at a flea market and this should be stressed, because the chances of finding the vendor of a certain flea market stall somewhere else after a number of weeks are small. And the organizers of a flea market, whether they be the local authorities or a private enterprise, are as likely to hold themselves responsible for a fake Rembrandt or Spitzweg bought in good faith at the market, as the city of Orlando would pay out accident compensation to a visitor who, during the Christmas rush, falls out of the ferris-wheel and thereby breaks a leg.

The flea market has wonderful charms which will arouse a finder's fever time and again even in a sober collector or searcher for rarities, and every now and again, although seldom, one can make a find or come across a really 'unique opportunity'; but there is no guarantee that one may not discover to one's eternal regret that much was paid for a worthless article, which, through a lack of experience, was thought to be a valuable antique.

Apart from the ambulatory flea markets of the mobile enterprises, one can find permanent flea markets in numerous cities both small and large. These are partly lodged in stores, partly in sheds, old garages or warehouses. They may just as well be called second-hand stores, except for the fact that their owners have simply chosen the name 'flea market' as their business designation, which is probably, in their eyes, more attractive and more nostalgic. In general, just as big a selection is offered as at most of the public flea markets in the open air. If it is not pouring, then they readily put their wares out onto the sidewalks, insofar as no local police ordinance

prohibits this. The colorful jumble of old chairs, trinket-boxes, vases and piles of records and picture postcards is for the passer-by just as attractive and inviting to nose around in as the sign above the window with the inscription 'flea market'.

Ten or maybe twenty years ago, such a large number of second-hand goods places as there are now in Germany would have been unthinkable and definitely unremunerative. The mentality of the population was quite different then from what it is now. People felt ashamed, especially in front of the neighbors, if the furnishing of the house was not completely modern. Nowadays, however, people consider it fashionable when one has the individuality and the originality to have the furniture, and also to be able to appreciate the dinner service, plates, toys, dolls or records, which someone's very own mother or grandmother used and to which she was attached. And because many people do not possess any of these things from their own parental or grandparental home, they go to where they can be bought: the flea market.

'Nostalgia' may be a somewhat worn-out word these days but it betrays something that is far more important and pleasing than a random fad or fashion, namely that people are thinking about the value of objects, which once, in whatever form and for whatever purpose, were made by people, whether for everyday use or for a festive occasion, or simply to while away the time. In no case were they made simply to be discarded before they were truly worn out.

Does the present love of flea markets and of used, but still usable, old articles therefore point perhaps to the fact that our world has become more human?

West Berlin
At the peak of the 'Jugendstil' in Berlin, like in Paris, a start was made to the construction of an underground subway soon after the turn of the century. This is why not only the interiors of the railroad carriages, but also the iron constructions of those parts of the railroad which were built above the streets, displayed many typical 'Jugendstil' characteristics. This could be observed most clearly at the subway stations in which, owing to the concurrence of Art Nouveau and technological architecture, buildings arose of which the historical value of the art and architecture only came to be recognized after many of them had made way for other constructions or had fallen into disuse.

Just such a 'Jugendstil' station stands on the Nollendorfplatz in the center of an area that was characterized before the war by the art and antique trade of the country's capital. From here to the Viktoria-Luise-Platz, one can find at present numerous popular antique stores and also fancy art businesses along the Motzstrasse.

Subway trains no longer run through the 'Jugendstil' station on the Nollendorfplatz but if one climbs the steps leading to the platforms, one can still see a row of subway carriages. The doors

Berlin-Charlottenburg
Klausener Platz

West Berlin
Nollendorfplatz

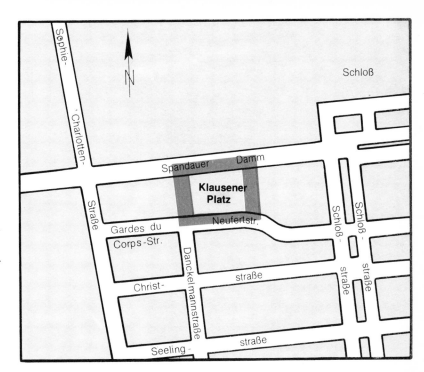

are open, the seats are missing for the most part
and, instead of passengers, they are filled with
second-hand goods, antiques and people wishing
to buy or sell these things.

It was an excellent idea to save from the demo-
lishers this 'Jugendstil' symbol on the Nollendorfplatz in the old center of the Berlin art and
antique trade, not far from the zoo, Kurfürsten-
damm and the Gedächtniskirche, by having it
function as the 'most original flea market in the
world', as it was called at its opening in the
spring of 1974 on the advertising posters. On
these it was announced: various antique stores,
second-hand stalls, a gallery, clothes boutique,
mini-movie-theater, poster store, black light
show, army stuff, handicrafts, coins, jewelry and
the Berlin Bar with Heinz Holl's summer terrace, 'Zur Nolle'.

Now vendors' stalls can be found here
crammed together on the former platforms; on
the two rails next to them stand two really authentic subway-trains, each having nine of the
oldest yellow carriages, dating from the time of
Kaiser Wilhelm II.

Objects typical of the time of the Emperor
dominate here as at almost no other German flea
market. Prussian pointed helmets, busts of
Bismarck which serve as inkwells, flags and
uniforms from the Imperial Marines and all
kinds of travelling bags as well as general kitsch
from the years 1871 to 1873 can be found, from
ashtrays with the Prussian eagle, coupling belts
with the slogan 'Gott mit uns', reservist pitchers
and pipes to a black, white and red striped original sentry box.

But this is just one aspect of the goods presented. On the platforms are also coat-racks with
second-hand men's and women's clothing, period
furniture, strollers, gramophones, baskets, umbrellas and all sorts of used household articles. In
one of the carriages, only framed pictures are on
display; in another, only Oriental goods.

The whole place has long been a shopping-
center for the Berliners, who do not always wish
to fit their houses out with brand new items from
a department store; but it is also a better and
cheaper finding-place than elswhere for the
visitors from Berlin who come across many a
nostalgic object reminiscent of the Emperor and

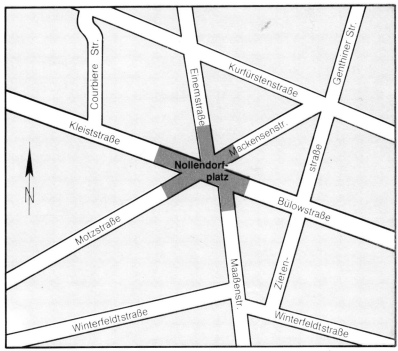

Flea markets West Berlin

West Berlin
- Forum Steglitz, Saturday, except in the winter
- Nollendorfplatz, former subway station, Monday through Saturday

Berlin-Charlottenburg
- Klausener Platz, Saturday
- Kantstrasse, corner Fasanenstrasse, Saturday from 8:00 to 18:00h
- Schlosstrasse 16, Saturday from 8:00 to 18:00h

Berlin: flea market in the subway station Nollendorfplatz

Above: *The Nollendorfplatz Market has an atmosphere all its own*

Right: *Some of the little stalls are situated in old subway trains*

Right: *Great-grandmother's umbrella and great-grandfather next to it*

Below right: *Might there still be a treasure in the chest?*

the Empire. Many things are very cheap and bargaining is naturally permitted.

The Berlin flea market in the subway-station Nollendorfplatz is open every workday. Other general public flea markets are held every Saturday in Berlin on the Klausener Platz not far from the castle Charlottenburg, and on the market square in the Steglitz suburb.

Frankfurt on the Main

Frankfurt, as you know, is situated on the northern bank of Main River , at least the old city-center was before it was destroyed in the war. To the left of the Main lies Sachsenhausen, which, since a long time, has formed one burrough with the enormous city which Frankfurt now is. But if one looks from the Sachsenhausen bank, aptly named 'Schaumainkai' (Main View Quay), across to the other side and stands eye to eye with such important witnesses of Frankfurt's past as the Emperor City, the cathedral of Paulskirche, the Römer or the Rententurm, then one can still imagine how the view must have been in the time of the poet Goethe or the banker Meyer Amschel, Rothschild, the two famous sons of Frankfurt.

At exactly the spot from which the view is perhaps the most impressive, the Eiserne Steg leads to the other side, a footbridge from the time of Kaiser Wilhelm II, which, in a war full of bombardments and blown-up bridges, remained intact. This bridge was always considered to be an ugly, disturbing element in the lovely panorama until people with the nostalgic taste of our day began to look upon it with more sympathy – and considering the concrete blocks of the Intercontinental Hotel and other skyscrapers which have shot up into the field of view, this is not at all surprising.

At just the place where the Eiserne Steg in Sachsenhausen leads onto land, to its left and right on the narrow Platanenallee until the following two traffic bridges, one finds one of Frankfurt's main attractions, the flea market. It takes place every Saturday and the bulk of the second-hand goods for sale here, kitsch and art works like at no other market, are things which have shown in the last years a rising line in the favor and taste of the public, similar to the Eiserne Steg, which can always be seen some-

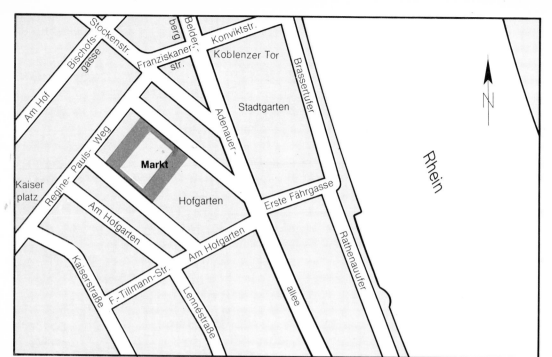

Bonn
Hofgarten

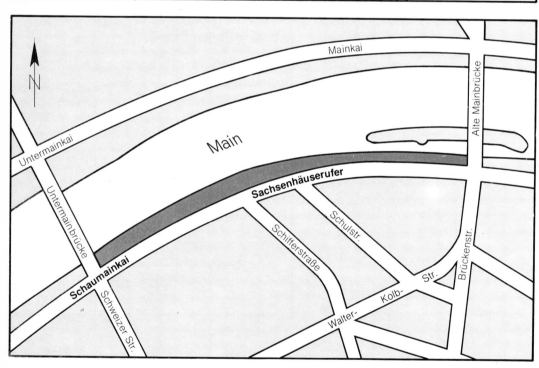

Frankfurt am Main
Schaumainkai

Flea markets Bonn-Göttingen

Bonn
- Hofgarten, first Saturday of the month, from May through September

Drensteinfurth
- Ortsteil Rinkerode, Monday from

16:00 to 18:00h, Wednesday from 16:00 to 18:00h, Saturday from 11:00 to 14:00h and Sunday from 11:00 to 13:00h

Frankfurt/Main
- Schaumainkai, near the Eiserne

Steg, Saturday from 9:00 to 17:00h
- Schiffersbunker, Schifferstrasse, Saturday from 9:00 to 14:00h

Göttingen
- Alte Ziegelei, Otto-Frey-Brücke, Saturday

where in the background.

Sewing machines with 'Jugendstil' inspired cast-iron undercarriages are also here; used clothing hangs on old coat-racks, children offer cheap paperbacks and domestic articles for sale which they have coaxed their mothers out of. There are sellers who go about their work in an almost professional manner and who trade in Biedermeier chandeliers, porcelain, furniture, clocks, glasses and paintings. Collectors buy, sell and exchange picture postcards, coins, dolls, toys, medals and records. Youthful amateur book-sellers, of whom it may be thought that they have just plundered grandma's bookcase, offer for sale whole rows of volumes by classical authors, bound volumes of Westermann's monthlies and novels which were well-loved at the turn of the century. Weapons and live animals are prohibited at this market.

When this flea market was held for the first time on the Schaumainkai, it was announced by means of a big placard on which the following could be read: 'Kitsch, art and junk – Frankfurt has its own junk market. Everyone is granted the right from the free imperial city from 12 August 1972 to sell whatever he wishes between 9:00 and 17:00h as was common from the fifteenth to the eighteenth centuries. At 9:00h, the mayor, Rudi Arndt, will open the flea market of Frankfurt with the sale of a few well-loved but unfortunately unusable personal articles. The Barrelhouse Band and a barrel-organ will be playing at full strength.'

Anyone can sell anything, in other words. You can display your goods on the curb, hang them on the nearest tree or spread them out on a table, if you have brought one with you. If you do not take up more than two square yards of city area, then you are permitted to do so free of charge. More space costs money, with which the city finances the cleaning up of the grounds; at the end of an afternoon, this is certainly necessary, when people have gone home and empty boxes, plastic bags, newspapers and pieces of wrapping paper are strewn everywhere. Sometimes also 'sellable' goods remain behind, which were probably of so little value that no buyer could be found for them and thus were left behind, because the transport home was no longer worth the trouble.

Maybe there is someone else, though, who

likes grubbing around in garbage cans and will find them and maybe do good business with them at the following market.

Hamburg

On the Elbe, where in the west of the state district of the old Hanzestad, Hamburg ended with the suburb St. Pauli, the city of Altona began, which first belonged to the Kingdom of Denmark and later fell under the Prussians. Since 1936, Altona also belongs to the big Hanzeatic sister city, but it is curious that in Hamburg there are two old squares both called 'Fish Market'. The first lies in the medieval city-center of Hamburg, south of the former cathedral and to the north of the present Ost-West-Strasse. This Fish Market was connected to the Elbe by means of a – now filled up – 'Fleth', (the name of the Hamburg city-canals which are called 'grachten' in Amsterdam and canals in Venice). The second one is situated right next to the former city boundary in the heart of Altona. At both markets, the Elbe fishermen moored their flatbottomed vessels immediately after the catch and selling took place from on board as well as via the stalls of the proverbial fish-wives of Hamburg and Altona.

On the Fish Market in the center of the city, no markets are held nowadays. On the other hand, the Fish Market in Altona, which the stranger believes to belong to the world-famous sailors' and entertainment area of St. Pauli, is, as a market, livelier than ever. It is held every week on Sunday from six o'clock in the early morning, thus long before dawn in the winter, to about midday. For many years, not only fish but also many other types of food have been sold here, including even live poultry and banana leaves. Often the goods are recommended in roaring voices. Because the visitors to St. Pauli, most of them under the influence, traditionally come and end their nightly revels over the Reeperbahn here, and because some visitors from the classy parties in the Hanzestad appear here after an all-night feast in their dinner-jackets and evening-dresses, the comic as well as the grotesque elements are never lacking at this market. Besides the fish and foodstuffs, all other kinds of curious articles have always played a role: old radios, cigarette lighters, records, all types of kitsch and souvenirs, or a cheap load of

Königstraße
Nobistor
Königstraße
Trommel-
Dosestraße
straße
Hexenberg
Pepermölenbek
Silbersackstr.
Kirchenstraße
Hein-
Hochstr.
Köllisch-
Erich-
straße
Balduinstraße
Hamburger
Lange
Straße
Platz
Seesternstr.
Schlachterbuden
Pinnasberg
Breite
Straße
Fischmarkt
St. Pauli
Fischmarkt
Str.
Rehder-
Buttstraße
Fischmarkt
Carsten-
Große
Elbstraße
Elbe

*Nosing around the
flea market with the
Hamburg harbor in
the background*

72

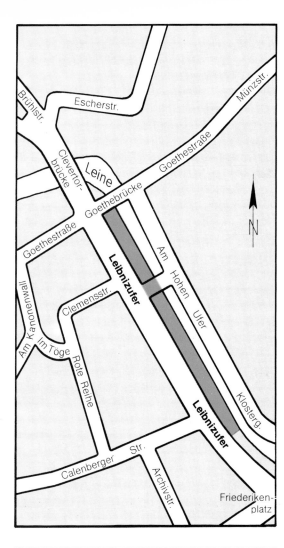

Hanover
Leibnizufer

Railroad market in Hanover: a paradise for train-lovers

Railroad market in Hanover: a paradise for train-lovers

Flea markets Hamburg and Hanover

Hamburg
- Alte Markthalle, near the Central Station, daily from 11:00 to 19:00h
- Hopfenmarkt, Thursday from 11:00 to 16:00h
- Flea market along the Elbe (old fish-market of Altona and surroundings), a few times a year, in the summer

Hanover
- Leibnizufer, Saturday
- Am Hohen Ufer, Sunday from 8:00h until sunset
- Railroad market, workshop Hanover-Leinhausen, a few times a year

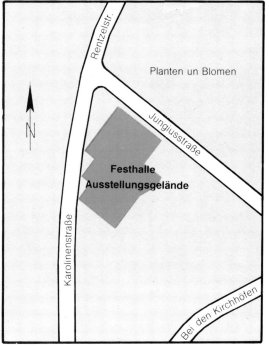

Hamburg
Winter Flea market

73

beeswax.

Before 1933, there was, in the Elbstrasse north of Hamburg's Michaelskirche, the symbol of the city, the famous 'Jew Market', an always popular classical junk market, which was held every afternoon, including Sundays, but then not on Saturdays, the day of rest for the vendors, most of whom were Jewish.

In front of the Fish Market of Altona, at the end of the nineteenth century, the originally competitive but later united fishing harbors of Hamburg-St. Pauli and Altona were built with auction halls and port facilities. In the last years, they have lost their importance as transshipment centers for the sea-fish wholesalers to Bremerhaven and Cuxhaven. But this entire area along the Elbe, from the harbor stairs of St. Pauli to far to the west along the Grosse Elbstrasse, including the old Fish Market of Altona and the streets of the former Jew Market, has for some time been the scene of a flea market through which, in a certain sense, the old tradition of the area is reviving. It is organized a few times a year in the summer by the dominating local newspaper, the 'Hamburger Abendblatt' and has become the largest in Germany. The advertising even refers to it as the largest flea market in Europe and, excluding Paris, this appears to be true. What stalls, wares and people are gathered together here is indeed astounding. In the background, the Elbe flows everywhere, the cranes and docks rise up from the wharfs and the long-boats and ships at sea glide past. The assortment of goods is just as wide as at other flea markets. It varies from furniture to beer-coasters and match boxes, used household articles and old clothes. But wine and smoked fish are also sold, and, of course, children with comic books are never absent. Besides this, there is here what one hardly comes across anywhere else: the maritime element. From sailor's souve-

nirs, ship's flags, ship-lanterns to prepared fish, captain's caps and boats in bottles; it is all for sale here.

From November until March, Europe's biggest flea market, on the Elbe, is not held. In its place, the just as busy Hamburg winter flea market is organized on various Saturdays, in a few halls of the exchange complex.

Market for railroad fans in Hanover
Whoever collects objects having to do with railroads can have his fill in Hanover. The German Railways recognized a tendency in this direction many years ago and have managed to exploit it. Worn-out items are carefully gathered together and are sold at set times for reasonable prices on the terrain of the Hanover-Leinhausen workshops. Anything that a railroad fan could possible desire is obtainable here: advance-signal wings, main-signal brackets, signs on which the type of train and the destination are written or which designate the non-smoking sections or say: Do not lean out.

Naturally there are also all sorts of lights, parts of uniforms of the railroad officials and helmets from the railroad fire-brigade, ancient typewriters and adding machines, stamps for the tickets and even transport vehicles.

Since the disappearance of the steam locomotive from the public transport system, reminders of these snorting steel steeds are much in demand. A few months ago, a young man even bought here a complete driver's cabin of a steam locomotive. He wanted it to complete his narrow-guage railroad train. A public gardening society purchased a glass control-hut which they set up as a kiosk at parties.

Something can be found to suit every pocket. Small train signs and colored glass plates for signal lamps cost one or two dollars apiece and headlamps cost six, eight or ten dollars. The popular red station-master's cap goes for five dollars, old typewriters on which it can be seen how well they have fulfilled their duties go for ten dollars and a drive-shaft sells for about fifty dollars.

It does not depend on the limits of one's wallet to be able to attain what one wishes but rather on staking one's claim on time. The first group of collectors is already standing an hour before opening time in front of the big iron gates of the Leinhausen railroad workshop. With perfect punctuality, an official opens the gate at the arranged time and the group, now grown to a considerable size, streams inside in a more or less orderly fashion. It is not unlike a sale at a large department store: the patient waiting suddenly transforms into a goal-conscious spurt; with presence of mind, people grab what seems to be of value to them only to suddenly capture something quite different from the 'treasures' which were initially intended to be seized.

To be sure, some collectors concentrate on one particular item which is still missing from their collections. They fumble about patiently in containers filled to the brim in order to come up with an intact manometer, regulator or watermark glass, a *TEE* sign from a special Trans-European Express, or even to find a very rare steam locomotive number. Whoever simply wants to decorate a basement, the kid's room or the garden shed need not grub about. The big signal boards and their two and a half yard wings, just like the buffers, which can be of service as nonmovable bar stools, are visible from afar; thus one can head straight for them without having to make any detours.

Dreams come true in Hanover. Hundreds of people come into possession of many very nice things within the short space of just a few hours. But whoever wants something really big, such as a locomotive that is no longer in operation, can also have his wish fulfilled by the German Railways. Only it takes a bit longer.

Munich
Munich has what one would nowadays call a flea market although it is somewhat older than the concept originating from the Parisian Porte de Clignancourt. It is the so-called 'Auer Dult', an annual market held in the suburb 'Au'. If one asks a Municher how long the Auer Dult has been in existence, he hardly knows the answer. He will shake his head, shrug his shoulders and say: '*Mei herr, des woass i fei aa need.*' For the citizens of Munich, the 'Dult' has simply 'always been there'. The 'Dult' comes just as the seasons do and no one worries as to how it originated. It is set up three times a year and it is the unwritten duty of every Municher to go at least once. There

is a 'Dult' in the spring, around the first of May; in the summer, on about the first of August; and one in the fall, at the beginning of November.

Even if most Munichers do not know anything about it, it is nevertheless necessary to mention briefly something about the history of the Auer Dult. The 'Dult' is mentioned for the first time in the city charter of Munich in the year 1365. It was then held on St. Jacob's day, on the muncipal common in the center of Munich, in the area of the Sendlinger-Tor-Platz. Today, an alley called the 'Dultstrasse' reminds one that here, long ago, the 'Dult' was once held. It was just as colorful and lively then as it is nowadays. There were stalls of dealers in silver and iron jewelry, habberdashers and upholsterers, purse-makers, bag-makers, coppersmiths, shoe-lace-makers, armor-makers, belt-makers, sword-cuttlers, cross-moulders, letter-writers, saddle-makers, shoe-makers, tailors, soap-boilers, strap-makers, brandy stalls, stands of the city cooks, biscuit bakers, gaming tables of the judges' footmen, tooth-pullers, stone-masons, travelling doctors, opticians, fracture-setters, root-collectors, magicians, sword-fighters, tightrope walkers, acrobats, musicians, actors, puppet-theaters and a whole lot more things which go to make life colorful, varied and a bit mysterious.

The common soon became too small for the 'Dult' and it moved continually until it eventually found the square where the people of Munich now visit it: the Mariahilfplatz in the shadows of the brick church, Mariahilfkirche, in the suburb Au, to the right of the Isar. From that day on, it thus became known as the 'Auer Dult'. That was in 1904 and since then, the 'Dult' cannot be imagined anywhere but in Au. It belongs there just as the two domes of the Frauenkirche belong to the city-center.

The 'Dult' is just as popular as ever. The huge old mirrors which hang on the many antique-stalls reflect the crowds of people who walk between the stands. There is no jostling anywhere and everything happens calmly and contemplatively. People come to look round, to touch or to admire the beautiful objects that are here, from the old petroleum lamps to the valuable bookcases. He who thinks that he most definitely has to have that Biedermeier chair or lamp should apply himself to bargaining because the

prices are usually high.

The price which the dealer first mentions need not immediately be taken seriously. It is possible to talk to some of the dealers about it. Only the buyer has to go to work carefully and tactfully, firstly by inquiring as to the prices of antique objects in which he is not immediately interested; quite casually he should then ask: And what does that chest of drawers over there cost? Enthusiasm should be minimized, which will likely lead to a price that is not too high. This asking price can then always as yet be discussed. This is as it is because the dealers at the 'Dult'

are not determined to squeeze out the highest possible price regardless of the cost. Most of them, like Maria Kölbl, who has an antique store in the old suburb of Haidhausen and who has been coming to the 'Dult' for some thirty years, says: 'I come for the pleasure which I get here. It is very pleasant, all the people too. It is my wish to be able to come to the 'Dult' for many more years.'

A time ago, when not everybody had antiques in their rooms, the collector could enjoy his fill here. One person once found many years ago two paintings hidden in a couch which people sus-

Isn't it a beauty?

He and she at the
Auer Dult

Now what does that
cost?

*Good weather in
Munich: the vendor
puts up his umbrella*

pected of being Vermeers, a gold pocket-watch
and a cuirassier. When the find became known,
not a single couch was to be found anywhere at
the entire Auer Dult.

But the good times have not disappeared for
once and for all for the collector. They are still
there, the precious coins, the sabres, the oil
paintings and the first editions of books. One just
has to look for them and have an eye for them. As
a matter of fact, there is something for everybody
at the 'Dult'. From a bird's eye-view, the 'Dult'
nowadays appears to be a sea of rarities, a Parisian flea market under the Munich sun. One may
get confused at first sight by the large diversity
of goods for sale. It is just like an ant-heap. Only
for those who focus their attention on details will
the 'Dult' reveal itself in its display of curiosities
both old and new. They will also find clothes
which grandmama once wore and which are now
being re-discovered by young girls of the present.
They will find razor-blades, tenth-hand pots with
ten holes in them, umbrellas with precious handles, pokers, breakfast plates, feathers, mysterious boxes of which no one knows what they
ever contained, clasps, glass-eyes, thimbles, key-
racks and many other wonderful and curious
things.

Obviously there are also the fun-fair people at
the 'Dult' with their wheels, little boats and
puppet-theaters for the children. And there is a
beer tent in which delicious pork sausages are
also served.

A small October festival can also be admired
here, except that it is more contemplative,
friendlier and human – more 'Munichs' in other
words.

At the center of the 'Dult', the earthenwaremarket is situated on long tables. One can find
ceramics, tea pots, cups with names on them,
plates, scales, cutlery or everything belonging to
a Munich kitchen or living-room cupboard.
Around the earthenwaremarket are the stalls of
the market 'screamers'; here Cheap Jacob established himself and sells ten pairs of socks for a
dollar fifty. There are also mysterious acting
gentlemen selling nice-smelling essences, medic-
inal waters and herb-drinks, which are guaranteed to increase the potency and promise faith-
fully 'eternal' life. Not a few Munichers come to
every 'Dult' to refill their bottles, because they

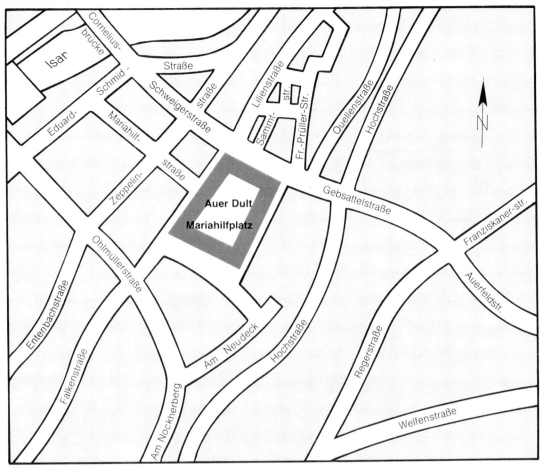

Flea markets Koblenz-Stuttgart

Koblenz
- Gaststätte 'Zur Krone', daily

Mainz
- Rathausplatz, second Saturday of the month

Marburg
- Plantage Steinweg, first Saturday of the month, in the winter from 8:00 to 14:00h; in the summer from 8:00 to 16:00h

Munich
- Auer Dult, Mariahilfplatz, three times a year for a week: at the beginning of May, August and November
- Between Belgradstrasse and Fallmerayerstrasse, Saturday
- Schwabinger Forum, between Leopoldstrasse and Ungererstrasse, Saturday, from May until October
- Theresienwiese, Saturday

Münster
- Servatiipromenade, first Saturday of the month, from May to October

Nuremberg
- Trempelmarkt, old city-center, three times a year, first Saturdays of May, July and September

Oldenburg i.0.
- Schlossplatz, first Saturday of the month, from April to December

Stuttgart
- Kleiner Schlossplatz, Saturday
- Marktplatz, Schillerplatz, Karlsplatz, Sunday twice a year in April and the fall

swear by the effects of 'their' medicine.

Munich also has nowadays, besides the 'Dult', a large, regularly held, modern flea market. It is open every Saturday, in Schwabing between the Belgrad and the Fallmerayerstrasse on the premises of an old factory. Many young people come here and one sees relatively more students than at comparable flea markets.

The same applies to the flea market which is always held on Saturdays from May to October, but then at irregular intervals, not far from here in the actual center of Schwabing on the Munichs' Freiheit. Thanks to the protests of the local population, this corner between the Leopold and the Ungererstrasse has remained unbuilt-up. Around the exit of the subway, a paved promenade was lain at the time of the Olympic Games. This so-called Schwabinger Forum lies beneath the street level and is surrounded by much greenery and flowers. On the days on which the flea market is held, it looks, between the flanking rows of houses, like an enormous, bright, colorful stain of old things, household goods, furniture, paperbacks, porcelain, silver, tin and jostling, crowding public.

At the much larger Theresienwiese, held irregularly on Saturdays, much of the colorful sprawling of the flea market is lost. This market has perhaps a more folk character than the two in Schwabing and covers only a part of the immense area of the 'Wies'n'. Only on the odd occasion is this area fully covered by the stalls, tents, stands, a few temporarily erected constructions and an infinite number of people. During fourteen days in the fall, no flea markets are held but the biggest annual fair in the world takes place: The Munich October Festival.

Nuremberg

When in 1971 an initiative group – comprising members of the city council, artists and other more or less worthy persons – spoke out for a 'Trempelmarkt', no one could possibly have imagined that it would develop into one of Europe's most important markets. The word 'Trempel', one should know, means in Frankish and especially in Nuremberg the same as 'junk' or 'old stuff'. It is a real junk market which is in other places called 'flea market'.

When the 'Trempelmarkt' underwent its fire-

Nuremberg
Trempelmarkt

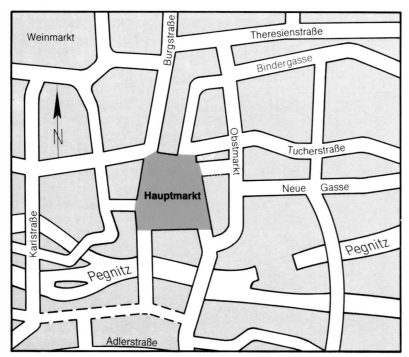

baptism and withstood it magnificently, one came across many people with original ideas. This market, and also the following three or four, breathed an atmosphere of originality. The market was set up with the basic idea that cheap goods should be offered for sale but also with the idea that entertainment and amusement should be offered. There was pleasure to be experienced everywhere at the market then. Here 'Pegnitzheu' and 'Nürnberger Wasser' were sold dirt cheap – no one needed to suffer from thirst. The musical background was taken care of by amateur musicians with guitars, lutes, trumpets and flutes and mostly young people who stood around singing together. On the square of the city hall, a well-known jazz group played on the steps and reaped much applause with its repertoire.

All over the market, an uncountable army of children offered the goods they had brought to the accompaniment of honest pleasure and passionate market-screaming. Then one could still make real finds and many a visitor who judged the offers with an experienced eye went home afterwards quite satisfied with the trophies acquired at the market.

A colorful scene in Stuttgart

This first 'Trempelmarkt' in Nuremberg was held continually on the first Saturdays of May, July and September. The official start to the market was at 8:00h but soon the starting time shifted to the day before while more and more vendors began to take part. Here is where the excesses began because of which the present Nuremberg 'Trempelmarkt' was to lose so much of its atmosphere. The first dealers took possession of their sites at 18:00h on Friday and soon a lively trade was taking place throughout the night.

This development was only possible because the market authorities, some forty overseers fitted out with megaphones, turned two blind eyes. No one cared a hoot for the judicial objections: trade went on the entire night regardless of the lack of judicial permission. It was chiefly professionals who did their business in these hours and left behind for the Saturday visitors a 'creek fished empty', as it was put by one participant in a discussion.

But these professionals were not only a big problem for the market, they were also an essential ingredient for its survival, which is an important consideration. In the long run, only they, by having a certain percentage of the goods to offer, can guarantee a reasonable supply of articles. Apart from this, it also appears that, from the viewpoint of one seller, it is more difficult to

Left: *The 'Trempelmarkt' in Nuremberg is held in the beautiful old city-center*

come by goods than to sell them. The diverse and interesting part of the supply could not be brought together or would not be sufficient for the collectors and retailers if this was done only by private sellers. Unfortunately, the timely possessing of a site by the professionals – in the previous afternoon or evening – crowded out those people who had determined the charm of Nuremberg's 'Trempelmarkt' for a large part: the clowns who came only for their own pleasure or that of the children.

And this is the image which the visitor gets after twenty successive 'Trempelmarkts'. The city of Nuremberg has not followed this development with much enthusiasm but it is nevertheless an accomplice to the state of affairs in the parade-horse of all the festivities in the old city-center, the 'Trempelmarkt'.

If one knows the international flea markets, like the Parisian flea market or the Portobello Road in London, then one can get quite upset at the activities at the Nuremberg market! While other permanent flea markets are mentioned only in tourist pamphlets, the 'Trempelmarkt' receives non-stop advertising. Success could not be long in coming. During a market, if one should cast a glance at the automobile registration plates of the vehicles which remain parked at a place appointed for that purpose for some forty hours, then one will see plates not only from the whole of Germany but also from Belgium, France, Holland and Austria. This is one of the reasons that the 'Trempelmarkt' is cracking at the seams. The market, which once took place calmly and where one could still wander with pleasure only some four years ago, is continually being raked up. Yet... a visit is still worthwhile.

Stuttgart

Twice a year, an extremely lively and well-loved market is organized in the old center of Stuttgart and once a year in the international exchange for collectors, the ISA.

The latter, held on the Killesberg, descended originally from an exhibition and weapon exchange. The accent of this annual market still lies on weapons of all types but chiefly on historical ones. Besides this, it is also one of Germany's largest coin exchanges and from year to year, a more interesting selection of curiosities and rarities and small, but very valuable, antiques are offered. In this respect, it is a sort of combination of an elevated flea market and a jury-free antique exchange. In contradistinction to other art and antique exchanges, not only dealers but also collectors – in other words, anyone – can hire a stand and put articles up for sale or exchange. But one is required, unlike at the usual open air flea markets and like at other antique exchanges, to pay an admission fee. Nevertheless, the number of daily visitors is larger than at the classic big art and antique exchanges in Munich, Cologne-Dusseldorf and Hanover. In the blossoming parks and public gardens situated high above Stuttgart on the Killesberg, the exchange halls of the ISA open every spring, from the Wednesday before Ascencion Day through the following Sunday.

In both April and the fall, a flea market has been held since a few years back around the city hall of Stuttgart in the old center on Sundays. Marktplatz, Schillerplatz and Karlsplatz stand full of stalls which generally seem to offer more reliable goods than what one is used to finding elsewhere, such as in the Rhineland. One sees here relatively many dolls and also – perhaps because of the proximity of a clock factory in the Black Forest – very many clocks, even if most of them are rarely a hundred years old. Often one may find fairly pretty baking-trays, cake-molds of zinc, copper as well as clay – a Zwabic-South-German speciality which one seldom finds anywhere else. Then there is, of course, a whole scala of old junk ranging from comic books to chandeliers, beer pitchers and arm chairs, from old gramophones to clothes-irons and fake Baroque angels, from oil-lamps to toy trains, 'Jugendstil' vases and cast hearthplates.

The rush is usually immense: some 150,000 visitors, it has been estimated, and the run for the best stalls, which cannot be reserved in advance, is well in keeping with the high attendance. Whoever wants to sell something should therefore arrive early, which is why many people come before it is even light. If one has been fortunate enough to secure a site, then one can still take a quick hour's nap among the pile of second-hand goods in the automobile before they get to be displayed and can be recommended to the fast-moving crowd. Twice a year, this is the biggest

Right: *Old books with extras: a charming tablecloth beneath and a charming vendor behind*

opportunity for the scholar wanting to get rid of his abandoned toy animals and picture books as well as for the collector who dreams of finding that long-sought rarity.

Less important and probably less rich in opportunity is the flea market in Stuttgart on the Kleine Schlossplatz. But on the other hand, it is true that one can try one's luck more often: the flea market is open every Saturday.

The large flea market next to the town hall is held twice a year

Laughter is called for at Copenhagen's Loppetorv,
or did you mean the Sinai Desert?
Beware! Loppestik is dangerous stuff

Denmark

'Everything that can be found between heaven and earth is for sale here.' This is the slogan of Copenhagen's 'Loppetorv', literally meaning: the flea market. It is located on a square in the center of the city, a few minutes' walk from the famous pedestrian streets Frederikborggade, Nygade, Vimmelskaftet, Amagertorv and Østergade, which together form Strøget, the shopping paradise of Northern Europe. The name can be easily remembered in a country of difficult pronunciations: Israels Plads, the Israel Square, is a name which does not appear on the older area maps of Copenhagen, because it used to be simply noted as 'Grønttorvet', the Green-market. After the vegetable market was moved according to twentieth century custom, to one of the suburbs, the square became a large, bare area in a not too lively neighborhood. With Copenhagen's feeling for humor and realism, after the placing of a sign 'Israel Plads', the square became popularly known as the 'Sinai Desert'.

The authorities tried for quite some time to instill new life into the square. An asphalt sportpark for the youth, a few benches and a speaker's chair were a few of the well-meant but unsuccessful expressions of the striving to create something with which the city could be happy. The building of a gas station contributed just as little to its glory; but this area also nurtures the automobile as the holy cow and these animals need to be looked after. The holy cows know mainly underground sheds; beneath the square there is a gigantic parking garage.

A few fruit and flower stalls formed a gay note on this square which borders on one of the big city oases of which Copenhagen numbers quite a few: H.C. Ørsteds Park. Until the spring of 1975. Then the injection took place which was to bring new life to Israels Plads and would drag it from its oblivion: the start of Copenhagen's 'Loppetorv', the first official flea market in Denmark. For years, innumerable groups had claimed that a flea market had to come and innumerable others claimed that it was as necessary as a hole in the head. And just like anywhere else in the world, for a long time absolutely nothing happened. But in a city having so much interest in crazy, beautiful, far-out, stimulating and undefined things, such a flea market had, of course, to come, especially when the Age of Nostalgia burst upon the Danes.

The flea market of Copenhagen may therefore still be young, but it has allure. It is one at which the Danish atmosphere can really be felt. Geniality and noisy enjoyment go hand in hand here, as is usual with the Danes. In a short time, the 'Loppetorv' on Israels Plads became extremely popular. From the beginning of May to the end of October, (and often until even later in the year), the market, situated near the former Latin neighborhood, buzzes on Saturdays with industriousness and the square forms the decor for the most colorful of theaters which a city can but imagine. On each Saturday, between fifteen and twenty thousand visitors arrive and thousands of kroners turnover is made.

Copenhagen's 'Loppetorv' counts some sixty small stalls, which are erected behind the fruit and flower stalls parallel to the Frederiksborggade. What there is to be found here is as difficult to predict as the right combination of numbers for the jackpot. Leatherware, glasses, all sorts of entities and non-entities in copper, brass, iron, tin and porcelain, gramophone records, a bellows camera from the year dot, old dolls, radios, mahogany furniture, grandfather's cocktail glasses, bread-tins and lamps lie in colorful confusion. And just as you can purchase an English policeman's helmet for 385 kroners, you can also find a knitting machine for 225 kroners, a well looked after piano or a rare old silver coin.

The most important rule on Israels Plads seems to be that nothing is regulated; but this is only an appearance. The Danes may like doing business in a somewhat messy, casual atmosphere but on Israels Plads there are definitely some laws. Barner Larsen, the chairman of the

Israels Plads,
Copenhagen

Danish circle of art and antique dealers, the society which provided the impetus for the market and which runs the whole show from a huge office, sees strictly to it that the ordinances which were passed by the city authorities are heeded. The market laws determine that only used goods, domestic articles and everyday articles of use may be dealt in – to prevent hoards of stolen goods appearing on the market; that every dealer's name and address must be made known; and that those who have a permanent stall lose their right to their site if they are not present at the opening of the market. The opening hour is officially set at eight o'clock but at six in the morning, the first articles have already changed hands. The official closing time is 14:00h, but in reality, two hours extra are usually added.

The flea market is especially a social happen-

ing. It is not for nothing that in the middle of the market there is a mobile bar at which the ever-present Danish thirst – and of course that of the foreigners – can be quenched. At this bar, there is a drink served which you will not find anywhere else in the world. The name: 'Loppestik' or 'flea-bite'. The composition is a strict secret, its effects anything but that. Whoever drinks one too many of the mixture containing, amongst other things, cherry liqueur, can forget about bargains on that particular Saturday.

Bargains or no bargains: a visit to this piece of Copenhagen is a wonderful opportunity to experience the delightful *couleur locale* which the flea market on Israels Plads has. It is a piece of folk culture which, according to worthy Danish custom, is rounded off with drink and music and in which once in a while clowns appear and musical shows are regularly performed. There is often much laughter but trading is serious. Barner Larsen: 'For many people, this market has a very important function. Take those who make candles or jewelry at home and offer them for sale at the flea market. Here they can get rid of their goods. That it is a serious business can be concluded from the fact that between 6:00 and 9:00h, there is a tremendous amount of dealing among the dealers themselves. They never get a better chance to acquire better goods.'

The success of Copenhagen's flea market also set people in other areas thinking and a year after its establishment, the city of Roskilde, some twenty-two miles to the west of the capital, could also boast of its own market. In contrast of the Copenhagen market, the flea market in Roskilde is open on Saturdays the whole year round: in summer from 7:00 to 13:00h; in winter from 8:00 to 13:00h. Place of business: the Staendertorv, the small square at the heart of this provincial city, which counts some 45,000 inhabitants, right next to the Dome Church with its host of kings' graves.

The flea market in Roskilde is an initiative of the local tourist information center and forms a part of the usual Saturday market. It is smaller and more intimate than its big brother but it has a good supply of remarkable and often still very usable goods. Also here the playful atmosphere is not lacking. The trade blooms amidst the sounds of a violin or a few accordions and, naturally, the beer is always within arm's reach.

Flea markets Copenhagen and Roskilde

Copenhagen
● Israels Plads, Saturday from 8:00 to 14:00h, from May through October

Roskilde
● Staendertorv, Saturday from 7:00 to 13:00h, from April through September; Saturday from 8:00 to 13:00h, from October through March

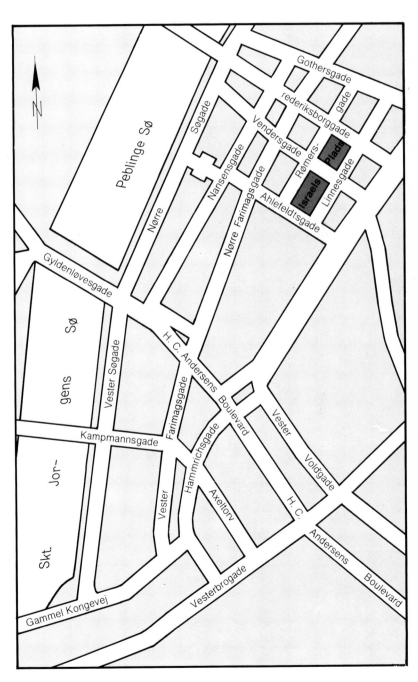

Copenhagen
Israels Plads

In Denmark the vendors have also fitted themselves out with a high hat and a cigar

KØBENHAVNS LOPPETORV

Hver lørdag fra 8 til 14
Israels Plads
(Det gamle grønttorv)

THE COPENHAGEN FLEA MARKET
Every Saturday from 8 to 14 a.m.
Israels Plads

KOPENHAGENER FLOHMARKT
Jeden Samstag von 8 bis 14
Israels Plads

Sunday in Liège: A good machine-gun pistol?
'Ah, Monsieur, everything can be arranged.'
Antwerp's 'brol' and quality kitsch in Brussels

Belgium

If it weren't so much work, the Antwerp author Fernand Auwera would have already set up long ago the Flemish Alliance for the opposition to the retro-rage (read: nostalgia). With disapproval on his face, he guides us along the disordered section of the market in Antwerp. 'You have the classical plaster pieces painted over with bronze paint: a half naked figure of a woman with greyhounds, an archer or a guy fighting with a bull, all very ugly. You could have seen these things at an uncle's or aunt's house I was happy when they were finally done away with. Now you see them for sale again. I think it's terrible, it is kitsch and it has no value. But people buy such things gladly out of sentimentality.'

At a safe distance from the crowds of sometimes shamelessly screaming Hollanders, who on Sunday mornings fill the Antwerp Oude Vaartplaats, the Blauwtorenplein, the Graanmarkt, the Arsenaalplein and the surrounding streets like squirming protoplasm, he declares from behind a mug of high yeasting beer his aversion to the phenomenon of stuffing one's house full of objects from yester year, whether they be pretty or not.

'Instead of people trying to change the society of which they disapprove, they go right back into the past. I think that's a pity. Everything that is now thirty years old or more is being offered for sale: objects are suddenly being endowed with charm because of their age even if they don't have any. An old coffee grinder, for example, can be real nice. But no one uses it; they fill it with old, dried flowers.'

The rise of the decorative element can be seen even in the building of apartment blocks, says Auwera sadly: in the form of an open fireplace, which is supposed to suggest something of the old coziness. 'If the family comes visiting once a year, then it is lit with much messing and hassling. There are people who switch off the radiators in order to have more pleasure from the fireplace, even if the whole apartment is then filled with smoke: such a fireplace is decorative – and aren't we living in a decorative age?'

That *diejen ouwen brol* (the worthless junk) of the junk markets has suddenly had a value attributed to it does not display any feeling for relativity, in Auwera's opinion. On the site of the bar where he met his first love, an apartment block has now risen. Regretfully: 'Maybe it was very dilapidated. I can understand how sad it is when things from the past disappear but that

does not imply that one should systematically follow a trend and find everything from that period beautiful.'

Once Black Jef stood at the market in Antwerp, an old, blind negro boxer. He dealt in 'jap' (pronounced: shup), as the Antwerp candy used to be called. There were also paralyzed singers and the old iron section was much bigger then than it is now. But on the cobblestones, one can still find a good lathe or an electricity meter. Non-electric clothes-irons are here, to be used as paper-weights. And for thirty francs one can have an old horse-shoe with which many an automobile radiator appears to be decorated nowadays.

The Oude Vaartplaats has lost some of its charm and atmosphere through work on the New Royal Theater. They have been busy for twenty years and the end is not yet in sight. Whether or not the theater life flourishes exuberantly, Antwerp had been promised a prestige object with revolving stage and for this the market has to suffer.

The Antwerp Sunday market derives the most fame, at least as far as the Dutch public is concerned, from the trade in birds. The prices are noted in Belgian francs as well as Dutch guilders. Winter-proof singers, little male canaries with a song-guarantee, incertine warblers or white-haired smews: people come from far and near for them.

The king of the Bird Market is chosen annually from among the vendors having the best gift of gab. Since recently, it is in fact a queen, a victory for feminism. The Antwerp market provides both dogs and vegetables. Typical delicacies: a sauerkraut sandwich with sausage or snails; scallops which are something half way

Above: *The antique market on the Hendrik Conscienceplein in Antwerp*

Left: *The Antwerp Bird Market*

91

Antwerp Blauwtorenplein

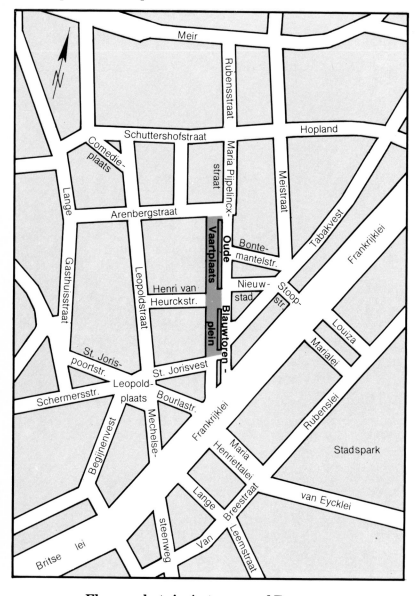

Flea markets in Antwerp and Bruges

Antwerp
- Blauwtorenplein, Sunday from 9:00 to 13:00h
- Hendrik Conscienceplein (antique market), Saturday from 10:00 to 18:00h, from Easter to September

- Old Clothes Market, Friday Market, Friday from 8:00 to 13:00h

Brugge (Bruges)
- Dijver, Sunday from 9:00 to 13:00h

The flea markets in Belgium have ceramics, too

between mussels and oysters and which are stuck onto sticks. The cafés in the neighborhood are also a treat; some of them are fitted out with old mortar-organs.

The difference between the café life of Antwerp and that of Amsterdam is that in Antwerp there is no chance of a dictatorship of the younger generation. Toddlers, well-dressed old ladies and everything in between can be found on a Sunday in one of the establishments around the Keyserlei near the train station. Whoever knows his way around Antwerp a little and desires to flee the somewhat too lively Hollanders at the market has enough possibilities of taking refuge.

Besides the Sunday junk market, the public auctions on Wednesdays and Fridays are attractions: on the small square in front of the Plantijn

Moretus Museum. Furthermore, there are dump-stores and pseudo-antiques, which can be found at 'brocantists' on the Hoog Street since the last few years.

Brussels
Grote Zavel
Vossenplein

Brussels
Early Saturday morning: the violinist, seen through the shiny window on the outside, appears to have fiddled himself to exhaustion. For an infatuated couple, he has run through his repertoire and now yawns. In the small cafés and restaurants around the Grote Zavelplein in Brussels (Place du Grand Sablon), it is still quiet. On the odd store door, a sign hangs with the text: At the junk market on the Grote Zavel.

On the way to the 'snazzy' antique and junk market of Brussels (for cheap knick-knacks you are subtly referred to the flea market on the Vossenplein), we pass the cigar palace of Zino Davidoff, something like Hajenius in Amsterdam but then, if possible, in an even more expen-

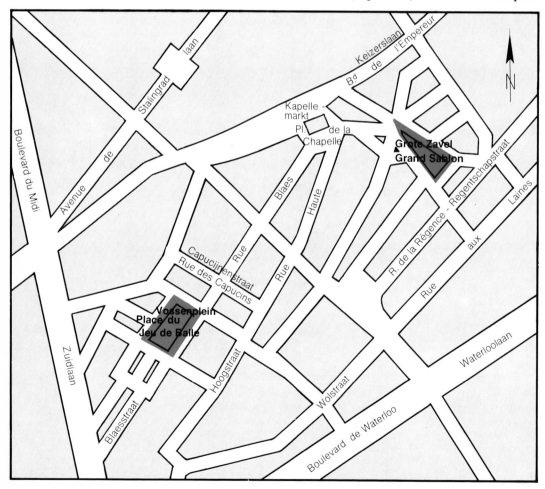

Art in all sizes at the Brussels flea market

sive price range and comparable with the Havanna-Eldorado Geneva that some people glorify.

The market is formed by stalls with red-green tent canvas, clean as a whistle, symmetrically grouped. On this winter's day, little heaters are burning here and there behind the trestles. A few vendors with red hands from the cold alleviate their boredom with a game of dice.

Almost immediately, the large supply of *Africana* on the left and right imposes itself on your attention: wood-carvings, ivory and masks. You may think that Belgium had not yet lost the

Congo, a reminder of the country's colonial past which, upon hearing the prices, is immediately chastised. There is much silverware (the zest for it does seem diminished), jewelry, chandeliers, religious pictures, old weapons (sabres, muzzle-loaders) and medical instruments.

Experts are of the opinion that this market's prices keep the mean between that of Paris (cheaper) and London (more expensive). And then you see one of these experts going into a neighboring antique store and pointing to a ridiculously expensive bowerchair in the store-

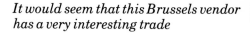

A haughty-looking doll

'Peanuts' is far more exciting than the customers

window.

The Grote Zavel is so arranged that the word 'junk market' does not have its meaning reflected. The prices: twenty dollars is casually asked for an ashtray with a woman resting on its edge; one with three little pigs is soon enough fifty dollars; a snuff-box brings in even more. The dealers seem less prepared to bargain than in other places, though as to the quality of the goods displayed in the shadow of Our Beloved Lady in Zavel, the collector does know what is doing.

At about the Saturday lunch hour, it turns out from one moment to the next to be difficult to find a place in one of the neighboring establishments which we had an eye on. We choose *Au Vieux Saint Martin* and snuggle ourselves among the well dressed public behind shrimp-croquettes and Filet Américain with French fries. Eating in Belgium is almost never a disappointing activity. In Brussels you have also a view of those ladies who keep their headgear on at the table and who are not seldom chaperoned by a creepy dog-animal fitted out with a coquettish mantle. In Brussels, the children impeccably transfer their forks from their plates to their mouths like pictures from a fashion magazine. Grote Zavel, the square with flair, the junk market without junk, the vendors with style and where even the fake does not seem devoid of class.

Flea markets Brussels and Ghent

Brussels
● Grote Zavel, Saturday from 10:00 to 18:00h, Sunday from 10:00 to 13:00h
● Vossenplein, daily from 9:00 to 13:00h

Ghent
● Beverhoutsplein, Friday from 7:00 to 13:00h, Saturday from 7:00 to 18:00h

Liège

'Thirty tulips for a hundred francs.'
The girl seems to be approximately thirteen years old. With her too short and faded jacket, she looks like a tea-cozy. Round legs protrude from underneath, bare and shivering. They have taken on a purplish tinge with the bitter North-Easter.

The little face is that of a madonna who has turned out round and whose goodness derives from the evil of the people who go to the market on Sunday but not to church. Maybe this is why nobody wants to buy her tulips. And yet her voice sounds just as raw and experienced as that of the toothless woman from the much visited stall for puffed chestnuts.

'Thirty tulips for a hundred francs.'
Her back is reflected in the window of a venerable antique store. Magnificent antique dolls stand ostentatiously. Some have a card saying:

Liège: 'A good machine-gun pistol? Ah, Monsieur, everything can be arranged'

Not for sale.

Behind the flower-girl, a youngster of about the same age has appeared. She has chocolate stains on her cheeks and grasps a bag of *boules de neige* and *boules de cocos* with her frozen fingers: honey-sweet candy. After a dreamy look at the window with the antique dolls, she approaches the flower-girl, takes a stand at about a yard's distance from her and begins to eat smackingly the balls from the bag, one for one, the face expressionless but directed straight at the flower-girl who is cold but sells nothing.

'Thirty tulips for a hundred francs'.

The little madonna head seems agonized. As the child opposite her, with a look of superiority and provocation, transfers the last brown ball with her sticky hand to her mouth, the flower-girl seems about to burst into tears at any moment. But then the tormenting spirit is suddenly grabbed with a rough gesture on the arm: 'Wo warst Du denn, Hannelore. Bist Du verrückt geworden?'

Hannelore disappears crying among the masses, dragged by a woman with steely eyes, wearing a comfortable fur coat and with one arm still free; on the other she has a flaky painting and a bag from which shining candlestick-holders stick out. The voice of the flower-girl seems more lively.

Liège. Three-country meeting place on the Sunday morning. Fellini should film it, at this turn in the Maas River. On the Quai Sur-Meuse, the Quai de la Goffe, the Quai de la Batte and the Quai de Maestricht, an aroma of fried onions and grilled meat hangs over the still sleepy city. On the left bank of the Maas, there are no more vacant parking places.

With your head still dozy – from drinking too much probably – flutter around Liège on a Sunday. A good way is to first 'do' the 407 steps that lead to the Citadel, a beautiful panorama, especially from the Cointe Park. A good walk via the Rue de la Résistance leads to the Pont Saint-Leonard.

At this point by the bridge, the market begins, picturesque enough with its lively stocks of mainly all kinds of poultry. But for the truly irregular of the real *Marché aux Puces,* it is still a few miles' walk on the cobble-stones alongside gaggling geese, high piles of pies, cheeses, sau-

Above and right:
*The Liège flea
market along the
Maas River*

N

Rue Hors Château

Place
Paul-Janson

Place des

Déportés

en Feronstrée

Quai   de   Maestricht

Pont Maghin

Meuse

Rue du Pont

Quai   Ste-Barbe

La Batte

Maas

Quai   des   Tanneurs

Quai sur Meuse

Pont des Arches

Boulevard de la Constitution

Place
Cockerill

Rue St-Pholien

Liège
Quai de la Batte

*A bit chilly in
Tongres*

sages, fresh French loaves, bakeries, art, kitsch,
a wealth of vegetables, footwear, pizzas, rabbits,
books, and 'a roll with sauerkraut and sausage,
Monsieur?'

In summer, you can immerse yourself in sheer
contentment behind a pint on one of the terraces
near the slaughterhouse and overlook the
squirming 'Italian' section of the Liège market.
Migrant laborers from the sometimes grubby but
never colorless industrial city of Liège (has not
the diligent Liège from times gone by been called
the 'fiery city'?) come here to get their *pasta*,
their olive-oil and their conversation from their
countrymen, where respect for them is assured.

On this dull winter morning, the clouds they
breathe out look like text-balloons from a comic
strip which disappear into nothingness before
you can provide them yourself with words. It is a
square full of people with shopping-bags, and a
surprising industriousness for the early Sunday
morning.

From one of the side streets, a cacophany of
whining and barking rises against the old gables: animals behind bars, stench. One dog can

do tricks on command from its owner. A wrinkled
old woman bends over a litter of fondant-pink
puppies with a show of much tenderness but
reconsiders.

A gentleman with a rough woolen coat, a Tiro-
ler hat and a red head screams in the middle of
the street at a woman with pamphlets in her
hand from the Anti-Cruelty to Animals League.
The Anti-Cruelty League has crept into the
lion's den. Right in the middle of the animal-
dealers, she demands an immediate cessation of
this form of torture. Heated discussions ensue
between the pro's and the con's.

'Dogs that no one wants to buy are put away. It
is a *scandal,* Monsieur.'

Behind misted-up café windows, the first of the
beer drinkers have purposefully sat themselves
down in the hope of some pretty fist-fighting...

Anyhow, on to the flea market. Half way we
bump into a statue of a market vendor which
stands like a beacon in the sea of people; his
corpulence is draped in a fur coat, his head
adorned with a mustache and an artistic hat.

He stands at the beginning of an elaborate

collection of art works. The man pretends with much allure that all the canvasses – and they are numerous – were hand-painted all by himself. However, they originate from the same 'factory' that has poured out in large quantities the scantily dressed little 'gypsy' with the inviting eyes all over Western Europe. The vendor reacts indignantly to the question as to whether he also sells any reproductions.

The smallest section of the Liège market is taken up by the lovable gentlemen of junkified and antiquated affairs. The actual Liège flea market borders on the Place Cockeril and could be called one of Europe's most remarkable flea markets. The distinguishing characteristic is not one of the most pleasant sorts. 'Moral decline', just like in the United States, may be kept somewhat stiffly at a distance but as far as weaponry goes, the Belgians are more free-thinking. Weapons? These can be simply bought at the Liège flea market.

The vendor has lain them on old rug upon the cobbles and there they lie : pistols, sub-machine-guns, guns from the First World War, and odd muzzle-loaders, bayonets, sabres, daggers and holsters.

Liège is situated in a border area, therefore you can see each and every week fat Germans handling with a nostalgic smile the abandoned weaponry from Hitler's war industry. High-school kids laughingly point a revolver at one another and with disappointed faces troop off when the price turns out to be too high for their budgets.

In the area of the 'weapons-corner', little information is provided. Someone reckons to once have seen among the interested onlookers some who would fit the vague description of 'people like the train-hijackers from Holland'. Another contradicts him warningly and with adjuration. 'Ah Monsieur, but of course it is prohibited to deal in weapons in Belgium. But the *Marché aux Puces* is not Belgium.' Besides, the police are probably busy with other things on a Sunday morning. So, what will it be? Light weapons of recent manufacture? *Brenguns* from the 'dump' of the Dutch army? If a member of the National Guard were to take a look in Liège, he would have a good chance of coming across the same type of pistol with which he learnt to shoot.

Papa fume une pipe....

Officially it is said that the weapons are 'duds'. But if it appears that you are seriously nurturing intentions of buying, then the vendor is quite prepared to help you come by any missing parts or replacements of parts. And the ammo? *Mais naturellement!* Everything can be arranged. *Entre nous.* On this winter day, despite the cold, arms-dealer Paul Diélie from Liège has made a job of his display. Beneath the bare heavens, he has carefully and lovingly arranged guns and bayonets between helmets and swastikas. It is no coincidence that he has much to do with the German public.

It is said to him how wonderful a gun will look

between the antlers on the wall. *Dekoration, was?*

Ja, ja, nods arms-dealer Paul Diélie and from the corner of his eye watches that nothing 'decorative' is lifted from his arsenal.

He is not inclined to talk about his trade, there is enough trouble. The newspapers can call what he does immoral but if he does not earn his keep with the selling of weaponry, then somebody else will. In Flanders there are cafés where you can get no strong drink – officially that is. But if you ask for a brandy, a 'witteke', then something must be wrong if you are not served one. And that is the way it is with weapons.

Something like a machine-gun pistol (an *Uzi* from the Israeli army is also available on request) is consequently priced quite openly at 2500 Belgian francs (approximately $220,–) in Liège. For a third of this amount, you can consider yourself the owner of a gun coming from one of the West European defence forces.

That the trunk of an entering automobile will be inspected on the Holland-Belgium border is a fact that is open to much speculation. Wild stories circulate in which the Rote Armee Fraktion, bank robbers, South Molukkans and future coup d'états play a part. Arms-dealer Paul Diélie

shrugs his shoulders and rubs his hands near the gaz-heater.

Someone calls out teasingly about consulting the feds. A name of a café on the bank of the Maas is mentioned.

On the spot, it later appears that one of the two patrolling officers has a hearty interest in the establishment and especially for the wife of its owner. Jests and the latest sports results from the RTB, while frozen market visitors from Belgium, Holland and Germany warm themselves with mugs of steaming hot chocolate.

An alternative looking young couple with Limburg accents takes a salt and pepper set from the holder to let it be admired by friends. Their purchases fit neatly into the framework of the revival of goods from grandmama's day. Even textile merchant Clement Scheifer, who is outside recommending his long underpants, packs his high-power sale's pitch in such lines as, 'Your grandaddy wore them too'.

Personally, we have come home with an enammelled coffee pot, which now houses a pretty dry-flower arrangement. Exactly: grandmama's time, but the price does not differ from that of Amsterdam's Waterlooplein Market, so I am assured later.

Whoever has the eye can discover even more at the Liège market: the bizarre charms derived from the inevitable tableau of Jeroen Bosch but then in a twentieth century conception.

Not far from the weaponry, a parsimonious little man stands behind a trestle with tin toy automobiles (made in Hong Kong), which can be wound up with a little key. He performs this work joylessly and attracts the attention exactly by not trying to. As soon as he has wound up one little automobile, and the thing is tracing circles on the boards, he picks up another one and performs the same ritual. Etcetera. He neither looks up nor around. Despite his sporting a poor mustache, he still looks like a child that for punishment from its father has to spend a few hours engaged in a meaningless activity.

He appears not even to have heard a little boy nearby who has burst into a complaining shriek of out of tune notes on a dented cornet he has just managed to come by at the flea market.

From the adjoining cafés with their live music (accordion and drums) played in a sort of terrarium, shreds of joy seep out. We still want to buy a bunch of tulips from the shivering flower-girl. But the cold has apparently driven her away, or, was she perhaps finally sold out? She has vanished like a puff of breath.

Arms-dealer Paul Diélie does not wish to say at the end of the market if he has done good business. He packs his wares up. Further on, there is clapping from a beginning café-polonaise: '*Adieu mein kleiner Garde-Offizier, Adieu und vergiss mich nicht.*'

An intoxicated man marches with a wry face and lowered trousers on the sidewalk. He salutes everybody.

He is unarmed.

A bronze smile

Flea markets Liège-Tongeren

Liège
● Quai de la Batte (alongside the Maas River), Sunday from 9:00 to 13:00h

St. Lambertus Woluwe
● St. Lambertusplein, first Sunday of the month, from 9:00 to 12:30h

Tongeren (Tongres)
● Veemarkt (summer months) Lakensmarkt (winter months), Sunday from 7:00 to 13:00h

Flowers in an oven; the pain of Waterlooplein
'Take a chance!' 200 year guarantee
Exclusive dolls

The Netherlands

'Take a good look around you. You can't walk past a single wall without coming across my stuff', says the vendor as he snatches an aerosol can from out of a dingy box. On it is written *Automobile Paint*. 'You won't get this off a wall too quick.' Exactly: whoever has a message for mankind these days simply grabs the spray-paint. Whether it concerns the Insect-sect, Reagan or the Revolution, or even the omnipresent purple slogans *Rather Lesbian* or *The Witches Are Back* in Amsterdam, the city-scene is sometimes a silent triumph for the anonymous people who let the walls, fences and gables do the talking. Scribblers have become 'sprayers'. On the Waterlooplein you can choose between colors which are less current in other places, as long as stocks last, or as long as the demand exists.

This also applies to the pieces of soap which were manufactured long ago for the Dutch Royal Navy but which never arrived. You pay more for a piece of it than you do for a new piece of toilet-soap at the drugstore.

Waterlooplein: the flea market of the unsightly, garbage-can ransacking hucksters is focusing more sharply than ever on fashion, since trendy Amsterdam purchased a 'far out' fur coat here and the whole province followed suit.

In the memorable 'Provo' [1] year of 1966, half of the 'pleiners' [2] were already decked out in generals' uniforms with gold lace, velvet jackets with golden braids and discarded footman's livery, all from the Waterlooplein.

What used to be 'dirty' has since that time been exalted by huge crowds to a cult, which does not appear to have spent its fury. *Au contraire.* The face of the trade is determined by it.

The old junkman with his rags, his dodges and his phony antiques has seen a young generation grow up slowly but confidently. It wants pants, jackets or complete outfits of military cut and it makes no difference if they are from the German or the French army.

You want to dress like a German sergeant-major? It is possible; and with a bit of luck, there is a Nazi helmet to match. You are a more sensitive type and see something in a Royal Air Force pilot overall? For sixty dollars it is yours... wind-proof and guaranteed warm.

Recommended as summer dresses and much in demand, East German nighties and petticoats with edges of lace and at least ten years old hang flapping in the wind. They are white, or baptized in a dye-bath and voilà: genuine cotton from the DDR where synthetics have not become as popular as they have in the West. It is the succes of the

Waterlooplein since the Grandma-dress rage.

The salesgirl asks a good twelve dollars for one. She is often found in a tailor pose on a trestle of her stall, young, business-like and the butt of gags from the public, (Hey sister, are you for sale too?), which she answers with a compassionate silence. With her mouth shut tightly, her head swings in nonchalant time to the radio's popmusic.

When she is not engaged in painting her nails, she is involved in conversation with an invisible partner somewhere behind a rack full of materials. With something of disbelief, you catch strains of conversation in a provincial accent on this summer day: 'Nice material I found this morning. Personally speaking, wouldn't have it on my body tho'.'

And then it becomes gradually clear that the square with the caved-in couch, the obviously imitated Toulouse Lautrecs, the rusty parakeet cage, the table with three legs, the brown postcard of the Damrak from the time that ships still sailed there, the Waterlooplein of automobile scrapyard king Jack Maandag (he is dead too) – in short, the square of the goods out of garbage cans has, with the arrival of a less cynical breed of vendors, acquired a different atmosphere. It speaks another language.

A new vendors' corporation with an eye for gaps in our well-being hangs its wares up, which comprise everything: the army pants are now called overalls and cost seventeen dollars; for a shocking pink or poison green dyed grandpa vest,

Coffee is getting cold in the meantime

you pay ten bucks. They are better and cheaper than at whatever boutique going – if the boutiques have them, that is.

But: shouldn't a jacket that you buy at the Waterlooplein be missing a button? Is the vendor not required to hand it to you to the accompaniment of a free commentary in a flat Amsterdam's dialect with an undertone of Yiddish? It is still there, but getting mighty scarce.

The new race of vendors is literary-minded and aid themselves with inscriptions in many languages *(Wir machen ihren Gürtel nach ihren Grösse)*. They are called Hilde or Onno and park disinterestedly their – let us say – old *Volvos* in front of imitation-brown cafés in order to join up with a group in which the code of behavior is determined by the sniffing of cocaine, little ceremony of words, the emphatic absence of peals of laughter and – in contradistinction to the jeans conformity of the sixties – a diversity of clothing: nostalgic accents, that it is surely, but then particularly cool and clean. Joy at the zero point and a glance at *déja vu*.

On the Waterlooplein, this decadence expressed itself also in the wearing of high, silk hats, copied from the Orange King with the tremendous mustache on the Albert Cuyp Market; the hunt for originality stops at nothing. In the left 'street' of the market, (seen from the Jonas Daniël Meijerplein), at the moment of this snap-shot recording, are still the so-called celebrity posters made from old photographs of film-stars – from Marilyn Monroe to the Marx Brothers. If the aspiring buyer shows some hesitation, he is told: 'Three and a half smackers ain't nothing – this poster can be bought no place.' One's anxiety about coming across the identical article in family circles or among acquaintances is never so expertly dispelled as at this market, by the same vendor who a few moments before was designating his wares as 'the latest rage'.

The desire to laugh fades a little further on at the seeing of boxes full of pictures which have been torn out of books. Fitted out with frames, they are sold as 'etchings or 'paintings'. The book-demolisher stands contentedly beside them, as if he has a heart for culture too. 'Waterlooplein, you long for the past. The many languages of your tourists, the verbosity of your vendors and the daily sauntering of your permanent customers notwithstanding. In you there is nowadays sold shining copper kitsch and materials which still smell of the looms, all veiled behind romantic names. But you are supposed to smell of the little folk, of traders, of the most unusable of Amsterdam's bankrupt estates, of copper cents. Your language should be '*Amsterdams*' with a Yiddish undertone, which you now do your damndest to preserve. Your gags must be sour, something to be gulped down.' *(Lambiek Berends in the Volkskrant of 25 september 1965)*

Now it is only the statue of the *Dokwerker,* the Portuguese-Israelite Synagogue and that is all. Nothing more reminds one of the former Jewish neighborhood. We even know of people who can hardly stand the sight of Caransa's concrete Maupoleum on the Jodenbree Street.

From those who returned to their old neighborhood after dozens of years, you can hear that they recognized nothing between the Waag and the Weesperplein. They view with misty eyes the comfortless, bare area where Amsterdam had once hoped to erect a city hall. The demolisher had just finished smashing the gable with the inscription *Stiefbeen and Sons,* a name famous both nationally and internationally for the scores of dolls, and which came into being at a time when the word 'playful' was heard everywhere.

Waterlooplein, a name which causes pain to the older generations. Confused images rise before their eyes: of Mose the pickles man, who came through the neighborhood on Fridays shouting, '*Karootje, wajewaje*', in praise of his slices of red cabbage soaked in vinegar; or of Semmie, who offered a cart-load of green cucumbers for sale but never mentioned what he was selling. All he shouted was: '*Ze benne als heipalen*', (something like 'They're just like telegraph poles').

(From: *Grass is growing on the Weesper Street* by Meyer Sluyser)

Pre-war Waterlooplein is the wrinkled little old lady with the trachomatous eyes behind a wooden bucket of water into which she dumps hard-boiled eggs. She peels the eggs just like a potato, with the back of a spoon. Pickled jerkins, boiled heart or liver, a few cents for a slice of coconut, the Jewish delicacy which should be

Bird's-eye view of the new Waterlooplein Market

eaten with plum ice cream. And slices of candied beets, Raffy Montezinos sold them in thirty-three for a cent a piece.

Nowadays, the people mainly want hamburgers and French fries. At the old Waterlooplein Market, you had a market superintendant called Van Ast, but who was referred to meaningfully as *Vandenash*. 'Nash' is the only business which is not washed out by bad weather. At Eddy's fish-stall, you could eat your bad mood away for three quarters' worth of tasty, hot grilled soft roe and spawn.

Now you have a good view of the absurd collection of still-lifes where grabbing hands make for a *tableau vivant*. Imagine the busts of Christ with the crown of thorns between time-pieces, old typewriters from which a few keys are missing, a lot of rusty skates, a vibrator (for all purposes – here for $5,– including batteries), a teddybear with one ear, a pile of hairclippers, a plate with the proverb 'Whoever growls has a dog's life' and an old man who shamelessly digs his way through a pile of old editions of sex mags. At home he checks to see which issues he already has, because it is a shame to buy the same issue twice, no?

Does the vendor perhaps have a pencil for him so that he can make some notes?

The vendor does have one and winks at the bystanders. He is of the school where haggling is still the rule. You cannot say that of the young dudes on the square: 'Theyz all store-keepers'.

The slight rancor at the changes at the market has not entirely dissipated from some of the older vendors.

Grumblingly, they have surrendered to the council's decision to build a new city hall between the Moses and Aaron Church and the Amstel River. Years ago, the architect Holzbauer came from Vienna for this purpose but because the government has not met the financially needy Amsterdam halfway with funds or permits, the square of the exiled vendors lies wasted in a neighborhood already heavily damaged by the building of a subway, while the architect inhabits a beautiful canal house.

The old Waterlooplein functions best as a parking place. Further on, in the direction of the IJtunnel, Waterlooplein '77 arose; artist Frits Muller was busy for days with gallons of paint to

put the name up as a symbol of its resurrection form the dead. The deportation of the market to a rectangular strip between the Valkenburger and the Rapenburger Streets led to an expurgation of some of the dealers, preceded by a genuine atmosphere of war.

The Director of the Market had ordered the vendors, like a bunch of school-kids, not to make a mess and made storage space available in the form of boxes and sheds. As the showpiece, the council assembled a few goods carriages from the British Railways which had been discovered by a civil-service employee on vacation in England. But with loud protests, the members of the Waterloo Society let it be known at numerous meetings that they did not feel a damn for being pressed into the shackles of a pretty street-fair.

Some of them feared, in the sway of 'Neatness is the supreme virtue', the definite end of the market, and saw themselves standing there neatly in a grey suit, with their surnames printed on a piece of cardboard and pinned onto their lapels: (Anything else I can do for you, ma'am?). Jop ('buy anything') Bouman, as chairman of the vendor association, spoke calming words to bring the tense mood under control: The market is now more surveyable. Experience has proved his prophetic words true – Waterlooplein new style, complete with the fancy girls in the clothing departments has become a wonderfully neat junk market.

Too neat, according to many a vendor. 'A street-fair of straight roads along which the people trudge behind one another like tame sheep.'

A certain Joop, who used to attempt selling television sets by the pound, (he had some five hundred in stock, all of them a bit broken), complains: 'Before you used to know one another but now I don't know more than half of them.' Behind a beer he loosens up a little and broods over the old square where sometimes at night he sacked out on top of perhaps ten tons of rags in order to be able to make a move when yet another drunk was out to rob him.

Okay, the square cannot be broken but the real business is coming back. Where can you still hear haggling? And about the kidding we need no longer talk, since the reorganization introduced a new business-like approach into the

Amsterdam
Waterlooplein
Market

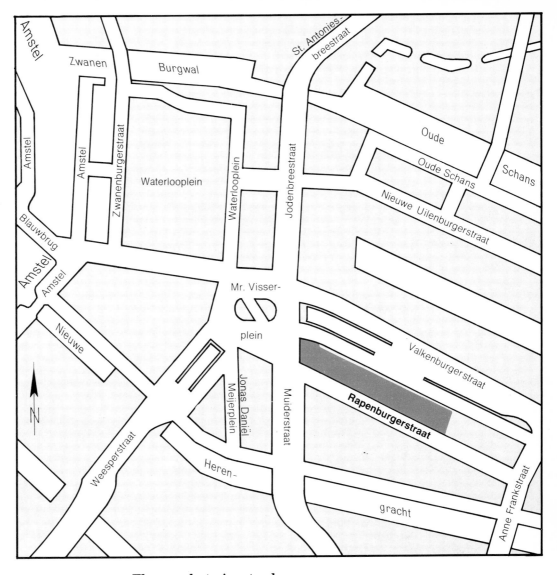

Flea markets Amsterdam

Amsterdam
● Waterlooplein
(Rapenburgerstraat), Monday
through Saturday 10:00 to 17:00h
● The Looier (covered
antique-market), Looiersgracht

32-38, Thursday from 10:00 to
22:00h, Friday and Saturday from
10:00 to 18:00h
● Noordermarkt, Monday from 8:00
to 13:00h

negotiating.

Gumption? That used to be the tireless voice shouting:

'First class pocket combs, guaranteed unbreakable.'

And then he would bend the comb so far back that it snapped, at which moment these historical words were spoken:

'The insides are just fine too.'

The only fruit-seller on the square could have been a model of the seller from the thirties who has been asked if his oranges are *sweet*.

'Well ma'am, I reckon so; they haven't complained once this morning.'

Despite all the pre-war humor and romanticism, the reigning poverty in the surrounding area could only be lightly camouflaged. Nowhere in Amsterdam was the situation so bad during the crisis years as in the Jewish Quarter. Already in 1901, an Amsterdam Council investigator reported that, in this pariah neighborhood, the one room houses accommodated usually five and not seldom eight or twelve people. The Valkenburg Street, along which the Waterloo-

plein '77 runs, was in those days a place of dirty
black misery.

On the neighboring Jonas Daniël Meijerplein,
one could see the Jewish beggars standing on the
steps of the synagogue (Shul) waiting for the exit
of the wedding-guests. A Jewish beggar was
called a 'shnorrer'. A genuine shnorrer should
not be confused with an ordinary beggar. 'A
shnorrer does not request, he receives. He is
aware of his important task in society, because
without him, the so important religious duty of
tsedoke, (benevolence or actually justice) cannot
be performed.

'Thank you' he never said; for doing your duty
you cannot be thanked.

'The authentic Eastern Jew shnorrer, the
Pollek, had more in his imaginary bag than his
Dutch professional colleague did. He was quite
prepared to allow his benefactors to enjoy his
sizable knowledge of Judaism as a much too
large a return for a meal at one of their tables.'
(From: *Memorboek, The life of the Jews in The
Netherlands,* by Mozes Heiman Gans).

The self-imposed humor caused by the position
of underdog and the poverty of the Jews still
seeps through on the odd occasion at the square –
humor with quite a twist to it.

The man who had the last laugh was Jantje
Smit. How he knew so soon that the Waterlooplein Market would have to move is another
story. But before anyone else got the chance, he
established a café-cum-coffeeshop, in a former
Jewish orphanage , which leaves you blinking. If
the new city hall, which the optimists dream
their children may still get to see, is fitted out
just as attractively as this café-cum-coffeeshop,
'Waterlooplein '77', then, according to the Great
Amsterdam Bar Book, from the year two thousand all the civil servants will go off to their work
with enthusiasm. Imagine, fancy gold wallpaper
and leather arm chairs!

In the meantime, there is now another owner,
who has no worries as long as the market is still
housed here. Jantje Smit has meanwhile thrown
himself into crosses and angels from Belgian
graveyards again and anything suited to the
antique market situated nearby. Jantje Smit has
done well and he began with screwdrivers.

The coffeeshop he started has in fact taken
over the task which formerly fell by its very

nature to the café, ''t Hooischip' near the
Blauwbrug. Little of what took place there es-
caped the clientele. In its protective cosiness, the
herring-vendor took his clogs off and raised a
song while newcomers to the market-gild were
weighed and checked. (Have you heard? There's
a guy with suitcases there who has done time. In
Marocco. Smuggled hash of course. Bought free
by his boss and now has to pay back the debt by
standing at the market.)

The Waterlooplein Market moved and arose
again; 't Hooischip became displaced.

Maybe you will come across that fire-engine
from the twenties in front of the new café, which
once belonged to the Vaals Council. Asking
price: ten thousand dollars. If your garden is a bit
too small to accommodate this showpiece of technological archeology, then perhaps you can make
good at the section wagon-wheels. Covered with
a plate of glass, a wheel suddenly becomes a
table.

*The Waterlooplein
Market: the public is
also worth looking at*

Under the motto, 'down at the farm,' a vendor traipsed through the rural areas and has more agricultural implements for you: scales, adzes, churns, butter-casks, spinning-wheels, pumps and, of course, the indestructable milk cans in which dried flowers look so good.

The flea market of our day is actually based upon the use of everyday articles for purposes other than they were intended for. It is not unusual to have a papyrus plant flourish in a painted ceramic potty, (costing seventeen dollars in 1978 as opposed to twelve two years before!). But a stove as a flower-box?

On Fridays and Saturdays, Jan Huybrechts and his buddy Wil stand at the market; two good guys from Klein-Welsden (near Margraten in the south of Holland). They deal in old stoves. Of the twenty which they sell, only perhaps half are used as stoves. The rest are purchased as 'decoration'. There are customers who let the sale depend on whether their flower pots with plants fit

into the round spaces where the pans are supposed to fit.

Jan has just spent three days polishing an old oven to make it ready for use. On the square, he has had a lousy day with nothing sold. Until an interested party arrived at the closing of the market. 'I could've sold the thing for three hundred dollars', says Jan Huybrechts, 'but I didn't want to sell it to that man, though I could really use the dough. But it's a stove to be *used,* not for show.'

A Brussels tiled stove sells for 450 dollars, an enameled flat-piped one for around two hundred to two fifty dollars: 'If you look for the wood yourself and go along the garbage dumps, then you can earn your money back in no time. Free heating... you can find wood all over the country, can't you?'

Jan and Wil have developed a recycling philosophy around their trade. They also sell rusty tools. ('We think it's terrible all the things that

113

get chucked out.'): 'Just a onceover with a steel brush and the thing's usable. One also has to be prepared to do something for them. With delight they can talk about their stoves ('some of these cost 150 dollars already a good sixty years ago.'), which could be found at some of the wealthier farmers. Underneath some of them, thick glass had to be placed: otherwise the legs would have rusted when the servant scrubbed and mopped the stone floor.

Jan and Wil purchase their old metal and iron wares from gypsies. The stoves and heaters often come from Belgian ironmongers. 'They are mostly guys who are quite intelligent. They are often a kind of sociologist. These Limburg oven-boys, (both graduates, worked respectively as taxi driver and in a clinic for mentally disturbed criminals) are sold on their goods.

A whole different kind of vendors are those men who assemble around the hut of the superin-tendant. They stand inconspicuously being con-spicuous. After a minute or two of reflection, their presence becomes clear. Some of them wear more than five watches on their wrists and one or more rings on each of their fingers. They have no stall, they pay no market premium. They peer through magnifying-glasses, helpfully shut off from the too curious onlookers by the environ-ment. They breathe on fourteen karats or imita-tion, rub little watches to a shine on their sleeves. As to the origins of their wares there is little said, if you know what I mean.

For some of the permanent, covered stalls, you nowadays need a retailer's diploma and an esta-blishment permit. Whoever wants an ordinary place is obliged to come at least four times a week. The vendor can no longer get out of it in bad weather, or, as the case may be, in very good weather. The show must go on.

Van der Bijl's antique stand has something exceptional each week: a 'sculptured' Mechel cupboard, heavy as lead, or an exclusive hall-stand from Belgium, or a magic lantern for 250 dollars.

Like many others, Van der Bijl rides through the south of England with his pick-up, not for lye-treated furniture ('that's become too univer-sal.'), but for rarities. Besides an 'English' cor-ner, the square also has a 'German' corner. Neo-Nazis à la Ku Klux Klan can have a treat at the sight of the display cases with military awards and rank-insignias, all dating from a most gloomy period. A selection of the present nostal-gia: an 'Elektrischer Schiessautomat' with the inscription: Exercise hand and eye for the Fa-therland; swastikas, SS and SD emblems. They may be gone tomorrow.

That which remains too long at the market without a buyer is given to the city garbage ser-vice. A youngster with an ice cream in his hand watches in disbelief as a whole living-room suite disappears with a crack into the jaws of a dis-posal truck. 'That is what is called the consumer society', his father says educationally. 'If you look around you can see enough things, even for the child that will be born a thousand years from now.'

Waterlooplein...Beneath the large awning in the middle of the market *(The Paraplu)* migrant laborers have found their place. On Saturdays, complete reunions take shape between house-hold goods and old clothes. Much gets bought as well.

Here you can find Bennie, who has been a vendor at Waterlooplein Market for more than forty years. Everything costs the same with him, ($1,75 in '78), such as: wrenches, screwdrivers, footrules and other tools. Bennie is assisted by two impudent youngsters of not even sixteen, who sooner get into a lot of swearing than into laughing. You will probably see them riding around in about two years in a 'Yank Tank', short-sleeved and quick fisted.

Waterlooplein. The former fashion designer and boutique owner, René Gerritsen, is a man that for a large part has made the market an attraction for everyone and everything that has to do with fashion. That is why you can find in Spanish holiday resorts like *Ibiza* and *Cada Quez* boutiques selling second-hand clothes coming from this square.

Buyers from the big department stores come along to the square in order to check out what the market is doing, and they buy their own collec-tions in according to the market trends. Only their prices are a damned sight higher.

René Gerritsen surprised the Amsterdam fashion world when he went to sell his self-designed bikinis at the Waterlooplein Market in 1972. An automobile accident led to the step; he

114

The Waterlooplein as it once was

had no longer the energy to design entire collections. Baggy pants, snow-suits, dyed baker's jackets and white evening suits: Gerritsen got rid of them all... and stayed.

With the advent of the Waterlooplein fashion, the first fitting-rooms were set up. Advertisements went: Dada, punk, junk-art, body-art, here a satin dress-coat (Yesterday's clothes) and there a flannel shirt for five guilders or two pairs of pants for fifteen.

The mellow-smelling Indian section (soap and incense) seems to belong already to the past. Contrariwise, the button is on the rise: round pieces of tin with texts like: *Enjoy Cocaine* or *Sorry, not tonight,* with a make of sanitary towel mentioned. Government bread coupons, invalid banknotes and textile coupons from the war also do pretty well.

Not all of it is equally nice but people do talk about the square – it is unavoidable.

Unjustifiably, it appears that young Americans wearing sneakers labor under the illusion that it is possible to buy a joint of hash or marijuana. There are less spiritually minded dealers, who, with a broad laugh, are quite prepared to supply American female students with a wide selection of obscene language. If they are not understood, they resort to international sign language of obscene origin.

They are the same all-time good guys who, after a thundershower, empty the pool of water collected on the roof of the stall with the unexpected push of a stick, preferably at the moment that a passer-by who has not bought anything is standing underneath it. The by no means casual exhange that follows usually ends in a nasty laugh.

The fame of the Waterlooplein often proves to be more reliable than its characteristics.

An elderly saleswoman of bedspreads and crocheted articles, which serve to enliven the window or the table, has found the solution: 'No, Missus, I only have them in white. But if you want a brown one, then all you have to do is to put it in *tea* when you get home; then it will look exactly like the antimacassars in grandma's house.'

[1] *Provo:* Youth movement in Holland which resembled the hippies and an alternative society.
[2] *Pleiners:* The youth who gathered together on the Leidseplein in Amsterdam.

The Looier
From all sides the dolls look at her. She herself is something of a doll, with a sweet face, tender voice and precious gestures. Her name must remain unmentioned as she prefers to be spared

115

the visits from the type of scum who beat her up and made off with dolls to the tune of some nine thousand dollars. That was in her store in the city-center. Now she tries her luck here on the top floor of the antique market, The Looier, in Amsterdam.

'It is really dangerous to deal in such toys, you know.' She has had to wear a brace ever since she left the hospital. 'But I'm carrying on, even though I have to pay a pretty stiff rent here. You have to consider it as a hobby, because rich you never get, even if the dolls are expensive.'

Mrs. S. has read some thirty-two books on dolls. As long as there are people, there will be dolls; they will never go out of fashion. There are some people who come to her and buy a doll purely out of love and thereby come into financial problems. Others look upon the purchase of an antique or Biedermeier doll as an investment.

The prices have risen through the roof. For a doll made of paper-maché around the turn of the century, you pay at least a hundred dollars. The usual prices are higher. Four hundred smack-eroos seems the limit but tomorrow the price may just as well have risen. At an auction, a *Bru-*doll (at the mention of which, the knower jumps out of chair) fetched some $28,000– not so long ago.

Mrs. S. also has a good collection of old clothes. The collector is usually quite prepared to pay seventy-five green ones for doll shoes made of old material. A real doll fan wants the authentic shoes no matter how ugly they may be.

As soon as some women's magazine has again spewed some tender prose on the doll-market, the number of customers suddenly flies sky high. They stand enviously near the display window where parts of dolls (made from porcelain, for example) are on show: arms and heads in a world in which tea-cosies and pin-cushions belong.

Mrs. S. takes the time to talk to her customers although reserve is also sometimes necessary. Here, too, thieves knew to break in.

Even the doll world has lost its innocence.

The covered antique market, The Looier, on Amsterdam's Looiersgracht, is, for collectors, a place to drool. Whoever might have had enough of the junk market and finds the trip along the numerous second-hand stores and stalls in Am-

116

sterdam too exhausting can wander quite fruit-fully among the antiques in this former ware-house.

In November 1975, the Amsterdammer Hans Becker crossed over from his bric-à-brac shop in Huiden Street, with eight other sellers in his wake. The public reacted hesitantly to this seem-ingly English phenomenon. A few years later, extension was even being considered (The Looier II) on the corner of Lijnbaansgracht and Elands-gracht, opposite the main police station.

The new formula was quickly adopted by the competition. Now Amsterdam is estimated to have some seven covered antique markets. Hans Becker reckons that a telephone call was made by the competition to the Economic Control Ser-vice, because the Looier is open on Sundays (viewing day?) and in Holland that is a no-no.

Left: A beauty, even if she is a bit cross-eyed

Below: Tiles, tiles, tiles

The officials arrived. To prevent the closing of the market, Becker started a letter campaign amongst the visitors with the idea of impressing on one's favorite politician or party that The Looier had proved to be an indispensable part of the Sunday daily life for the country.

The furniture costs between fifty and five thousand dollars, and dates from 1850, with once in a while a piece from an even earlier period. Fragile champagne glasses change hands for $225– for twelve. 'I've just sold twelve to a girl-friend of *Fong Leng*', remarks Hans Becker, heedlessly flirting with his relations in the fash-ion world. Notwithstanding, the aspiring buyer has to think about things for a few moments.

Becker has more expensive glassware. For example, vases from the French glass-artist Emile Gallé cost between $325 and $6500. No market like this one to rub your eyes.

The Looier, with its earthenware toilet-chain handles, a cookie-tin with a picture of Astrid, the former Belgian ruler, is more in the nature of a junk market. For private persons, there is the opportunity to sell their own goods once a month on Saturdays. This is called the *vrijmarkt* or 'free market.'

The ordinary market is held on Thursdays (10:00 to 22:00h), on Fridays and Saturdays (10:00 to 18:00). 'I get dealers from all over the world offering me things. They know I buy for reasonable prices,' explains Hans Becker self-confidently. The scarcity of the article deter-mines its price, or, in actual fact, the big auction firms Sotheby's and Christie's in Engeland do. 'And if you work a bit under the prices, then you sell.' Does Becker never foresee a decline in the collector's spirit?

He does not think so. You always have a senti-mental feeling for things which, through the renovation rage, have been in danger of disap-pearing. 'The museums are most stimulating', he says, 'and for a large part of the public, buying antiques and curiosities is a good way of covering inflation.'

Restorers and professionals from the Rijksmu-seum can find just that old tool for which they have been looking for so long.

As collector's objects, an assembly of old gra-mophones, sewing equipment, naval stuff, clocks and ceramics catch the eye. What can one think

The newspaper cannot be missed even for a day

of an eighteenth-century painted bob-sled selling for five hundred dollars? Not exactly junkyard prices.

Closer to home, both in price and in period of origin, are the hat pins: an article that has to be watched sharply.

And it will not take long before the objects of more recent times take the place of the rarities. The 'Art trade' says so itself. The Picasso-style furniture from the fifties is now having its turn; I am assured this by the people from The Looier.

And saturated with this knowledge, you

search, you peer, you riffle, you miss, curse and rejoice. Where? At the genuine uncovered flea market.

Not so?

Noordermarkt

If at Amsterdam's Noordermarkt a theology student keeps the watch dreamily over out-dated lingerie, creased soft-porno books and socialistic revolutionary literature, then this cannot be called astonishing. Twenty- or thirty-year olds,

On the buzz-bike to the 'Plein'

with a philosophic eye and conversation to match, are regularly found here. The charm of the Noordermarkt is not that it is situated in the heart of the Jordaan area but that the junk-section is partly manned by non-professional vendors: for a moderate price, anyone who wants to can stand at this market, and intellectuals in need of money, students wanting to get rid of their old books and girl-friends who have together plucked their wardrobes bare and sift through the clothes which are no longer worn, all stand at the market. You can grub about among old clothes costing two quarters a piece. Or for twice that amount, you can snatch the faded glory of a wedding-outfit from off of the kerb-stones.

The Noordermarkt is, as is often the case in Holland and Belgium, a combination of a regular market and a flea market. The pleasantness is reinforced by the presence of cafés. When the market closes at one o'clock, café Huisman is just opening. People from the Jordaan keep the tradition alive by filling the little upstairs room with children. Until a few years ago, they were served by the only innkeeper in Amsterdam decked out

with a Scottish checkered sweater and pipe. With tears in his eyes, he handed his business over to his successor.

The vendors of the Noordermarkt refresh themselves in the café De Wester in Wester Street. On Mondays, the market-visitor will once in a while want to whip into the café 't Smakzeyl on the other side of the Prinsengracht. (Speciality: Toasted beef sandwiches with baked potatoes inside).

Whoever happens to be lucky, may chance across an egg-seller mumbling to himself. He is called Sjors, is small in stature and inhabits a director's hut on a remote piece of bare land in the Western Harbor Area. He has been living there for as long as people can remember, protected by terrifying dogs. He prides himself that the chickens which scratch around in the sand by the hut are feeding themselves on 'pure nature'.

The eggs which Sjors sells are packed in lots of newspaper. Yolk, shit, feathers and fluff form the trade-mark against which no chicken-battery can compete. If you are unable to find Sjors on the Noordermarkt, you can always try at the Lindengracht.

119

Left: *The Grote Markt in Groningen*

Below: *The guys also play with dolls in Groningen*

Groningen

There are some dealers who do not give a damn what they sell. If their trade goes bust, then they change without shedding a tear to flower-pots or French fries. Earning money is more important to them than good vibes.

This mentality reflects itself in the copperware section. For the enhancement of their living quarters, crowds of people arrive at the dealer in copper decorative wares.

'Is that old, vendor?'

'Well, Missus, it wasn't made yesterday. You can see that easily, can't you?'

On arriving at home, it appears that the year 1976 is engraved in tiny letters. So back to the market. Then the vendor says:

'But Missus, did you ever hear me say that it was antique?'

There are obviously not enough manifestations of regret to cause the copper bosses to split the scene: customer's own fault. Antique copper appears in nine out of ten cases to originate from that one factory in Haarlem (near Amsterdam) and there they make no bones about shorter working hours. The Grote Markt in Groningen provides a blushing example of this time and again.

Its dubious fame has, in that respect, not remained unobserved beyond the country's borders: *'Groningen? Aber da gibt es doch nur Neues Kupfer, nicht?'* according to an antique boss from the Berlin Nollendorfplatz who laughs scornfully. He obtained his information from countrymen who visit Groningen regularly.

But the two Groningen junk markets have not been done complete justice with these remarks. The beautifully situated market square does house plenty of life and color, otherwise the surrounding cafés do. There is enough at hand in which to nose around: furniture, domestic articles and books.

Permanent features (as they both fervently wish) are two young men from Limburg in the south, who deal in old stoves, farm heaters and rusty agricultural implements. They propagate the necessary rule of the thumb that a client ought to be an artisan and must be able to replace missing parts or repair defective ones himself. A stove is not just for decoration, is it? (See also under *Waterlooplein, Amsterdam*).

Sign language

The Hague

Sunday morning in the Herman Coster Street in The Hague's Schilderswijk.

A few dealers in somewhat better goods bordering on genuine antiques stand together in a stall. There is not much to be earned. Once in a while, a passer-by inquires as to the price of an oval mirror or an old mahogany cupboard. As soon as the vendor mumbles boredly a figure with two or three zeros, the customer shrinks visibly a bit and continues his way a little 'shamefacedly'.

'You know what it is, boys?' says the one vendor in a ringing Hague accent, 'these goods of ours are getting much too expensive. The people who come here are all two hundred in the week types. The better public you don't see here, they go to the Voorhout.'

'Might be', says a heavy-set colleague, 'but it's real nice here on Saturdays, isn't it?'

And he is right. The silent gentility of Upper The Hague is out of sight at the flea market behind the Hobbemaplein. Here those people buy who want their quarters to be worth bucks. The Hague's flea market, unlike many others, is part of the large Saturday market. Whoever has already bought his fruit and vegetables can wander for a while along the long row of stalls full of goods which have been discarded or sold through necessity.

The combination of both new and old goods and junk has its advantages. One can always be assured of a pleasant bustle. It begins in a folk café, Willy, on the corner of the Herman Coster Street, where an Antwerp-like atmosphere pervades. But much Saturday morning pleasure abounds in other places as well. Go and take a look at the 'Chicken Soup Tent' (the 'oldest address') or mingle among the eager customers at the pancake stall where they bake very tasty golden brown L.P.'s for a few dimes.

Lost your child? No problem. A warm, honey-sweet voice requests every few moments a mother to report to the market building, 'where your daughter is waiting for you'.

A somewhat dispirited man attempts to sell fiery paintings of gypsy girls beneath a large sign which advertises 'Buttersoft Beef'.

A dark odds and ends stall seems, according to the inscription, to be the property of one Kafka from the Spinoza Street. A woman who sells clothing from the old days answers to the name 'Eline'.

Incredible is the interest in a cozy stall full of old books, magazines and comic strips. Especially items in the last category fly over the counter. A young boy asks the price of a pound of 'Kid Colts'. 'Two-fifty', says the vendor. The

Still-life with gramophone, typewriter and family portrait

Flea markets Arnhem-Utrecht

Arnhem (G)
- Kerkplein, Friday, from 8:30 to 13:00h

Groningen (Gr)
- Grote Markt, Wednesday and Thursday from 9:00 to 17:00h; Saturday from 9:00 to 18:00h

The Hague (ZH)
- Herman Costerstraat, Monday, Friday and Saturday from 8:00 to 18:00h

's Hertogenbosch (Bois-le-Duc) (NB)
- St. Janskerkhof, first Sunday of the month from 12:00 to 17:00h

Rotterdam (ZH)
- Binnenrotte, Tuesday and Saturday from 10:00 to 17:00h

Utrecht (U)
- Vredenburg, Saturday from 7:00 to 14:00h

same amount of 'Agent X's' cost only two bucks: a dealer with a feeling for quality.

He is timidly approached by a gentleman who looks as if he has seen better times. The man inquires if the vendor also buys books and if he does so at his private address. 'I have a pretty good hoard lying about which I would like to get rid of, through circumstances', the man clarifies.

'It's possible', growls the vendor, 'a quarter a piece.'

After reading the disappointment on the man's face, he says carelessly: 'Now listen here you. I can buy them for a hundred smackers a ton from the Salvation army. So you just go on and figure it out.'

One can easily reach the market by streetcar (Hobbemaplein). Those coming by car can most likely find parking space in one of the surrounding streets.

Above left: *Reflection in The Hague*

Left: *Had enough of the permanent wash basin? Buy a water-jug then*

Above: *Things are cheap in The Hague*

Real creepies

How is it that one hears so little shouting at the flea market in Rotterdam? It is one of the biggest in The Netherlands and certainly not one of the least pleasant.

Bertus de Graaf knows all about it. We meet him while looking for a light for a smoke. He is leaning against a pillar of the viaduct under which the junk market of the Maas River city is assembled in rows. He comes here every Saturday morning, at least if the weather is okay. 'Then I buy something small for my wife, because she's crazy about those copper things. After that, I stand around at my leisure just watching. At about half past twelve I go and get a couple of smoked eels and then I go on home.'

Bertus is a doorman and so he reckons he knows something about human nature. His trained eye sees that the visitors are just about all Rotterdamers or 'brown people who work here'. In the summer, there are naturally tourists as well but people from the other cities come but seldom to the Rotterdam market. 'I have been about three times to the Waterlooplein Market in Amsterdam and there you see people from all over the country. People talk to one another and so a market gets a big name.'

Bertus de Graaf points out yet another difference: 'I have visited many Dutch markets, because I like the atmosphere, but no place do you see people stuffing themselves with food like here in Rotterdam. Just look around you: they walk about eating or stand in rows waiting to buy. I've never seen so many food-stalls as there are here.'

The Rotterdam flea market is open from 10:00 to 17:00h and is situated on the Binnen Rotte, near the Grote Markt, beneath the incense of the Sint Laurens Church. If you come by car, then you should bear in mind that parking in the immediate vicinity is pure desperation. The center of Rotterdam on a Saturday morning is jam-packed. A parking garage for automobiles in the area has room for about four to five hundred of them, but one will have to be prepared to wait in a long queue until some market-visitor has finished doing his buying. It is thus sensible to park your automobile at some distance from the Laurens Church.

Dominant articles at the Rotterdam market

are old gramophone records and second-hand clothes. These draw a lot of attention. We come across an elated woman coming out of a stall with seven charming dresses and three fine pairs of jeans. It is Easter Saturday and we heard by chance that she had eight children at home.

In a nearby stall, a violent argument is raging over the books between a scraggy vendor and a beany customer with glasses. He wants to know what a book of poetry by Heinrich Heine costs.

'Ten guilders'.

'Whaaat?'

'Ten guilders. That there is a real fine book my boy. That's not just any old crap, that's Heine. You ain't never hoid of Heine?'

'Of course I have, but it's damn expensive.'

'Expensive? Expensive? Maybe ya oughta buy a paperback on the Lijnbaan, cost ya at least twelve bucks. Man, just piss off outa here. Even if ya offered me fifty bucks, ya aint worth this book.' The beany slinks off but remains hanging around in the area of the stall. When he gets a bit too close a little later, the vendor, turned all red, screams: 'If ya don't piss off now then I'll tell the cops that ya wanted Heine for nuttin'.'

More peaceful scenes take place at a cosy happening where puppies and rabbits can be bought. The children are not to be dragged away. Parents get desperate because the kids want a rabbit in the apartment regardless. 'That's just not possible, Michel', a bearded father instructs. 'We don't have enough space for it.' The kid begins to whine that there is enough space for two in his bed and if that is not enough, then they can always chuck the t.v. out.

'Which would you like? Don't you think that this one here is real pretty?' the vendor amiably interjects completely ignoring the agony of the parents. On the counter, he has a baby-rocker on which he keeps placing a different animal. An almost irresistable seller's trick supported by the whine of the small puppies who jump up against the wire mesh of their cages in order to draw attention to their distressful plight; but Rotterdam has unfortunately only a few homes with gardens and is not richly covered with forest or field.

Children grow up. The dealer in military articles knows that. At about fifty yards from the pets, he has his array of wares displayed on the street age-old weapons, helmets, caps, insignias, badges, awards, uniforms and boots. In the center lies the hardest pornography in the world: a bound volume of *Volk en Vaderland*.

His best clients (the official Dutch Nazi paper in WWZ) are boys of high-school age. 'Mister, how much does that knife cost?'

'Two hundred guilders. It's a Maroccan Djambola, two hundred years old.'

That figures then.

'And that cap there, huh?' He points to a German cap, which even without a head sends shivers up one's spine.

'That one's fifty guilders (twenty-five dollars): genuine German.'

'And what's the cheapest that you got?' the child persists.

It turns out that he is able to gain possession of an eagle insignia for seven guilders fifty. He has that amount exactly.

'Won't be able to buy no fries', his buddy warns him.

'So what?' he answers happily. The collection of the vendor is conspicuously German. Whoever experienced the Second World War can rediscover all the attributes of his terror on this square yard of Rotterdam street.

'The Allied stuff don't sell on the street', reveals a vendor, who would rather not mention his name. 'German articles sell like hot cakes, whether it be boots or caps. Even for a rusty gasoline can they are prepared to pay good money, as long as it came from the Nazis. And that's the way it is with everything. The more hated the country of origin, the better it sells.'

A Dutch army jacket from the Second World War costs thirty-eight dollars, a German one costs double that. The Dutch one is not only nicer but is also in better shape. What determines the prices?

'The collectors', replies the vendor. After the war he himself began as a collector and everyone thought he was nuts. At a given moment, he had collected so much of the stuff that he began trading. Besides that, he got into in repairing old weapons. He has earned a pretty decent living like this.

'Mister, what does that pistol cost?'

'Hundred and fifty, dates from 1813. Transposed from flint to percussion', he says academi-

*This gentleman
from Rotterdam
knows all about it*

*Cycling is also
common in
Rotterdam*

cally. A South Molukkan buys a Cuban parachutist pin and proudly shows it to his white girlfriend. The school-kids continue their questioning:

'What do those boots cost? Is that a German helmet?' ('No, it's Canadian'). 'Oh. And that jacket, is that German? Why is there a hole in that helmet, huh? Is that a cap from the Africa Corps?'

This machine-gun-like questioning of the boys is answered in detail. Then he says: 'These kids aren't good business. I have to make good with permanent customers who are usually adults. And they all go for that Nazi stuff. The interest in it is growing by the day.'

A pair of officer's boots appears to cost less than the men's boots. Why?

'Because the officers looked after their equipment. They were proud of their uniforms, hung them up and so on after duty. After the war, one could find plenty. The men's uniform were either lost or went for a trifle to the dump.'

A boy of at the most fifteen, dressed in a soldier's jacket with German awards on it, points out a pistol for us that he wants to buy.

'I've been saving two months now for it and I reckon I can buy it in a few weeks time. Just checking to see that it's still here.'

A little further, a somewhat older fellow is standing proudly behind his own stall. His bicycle leans against the side, decorated with a flag from the local soccer club. On his three square yards of wooden stall, he has dozens of signs displayed which one usually finds on the back of an automobile and which announce to the world all the extras which that particular automobile has: 'GT', 'Injection', '200SL', 'Automatic', 'Sprint Coupé' and so on. First class status symbols.

The question arises as to how he comes by them. But what does it matter?

As long as he does not buy a German cap from the profit it is all okay.

The charm of the Portobello Road. Good trade in bad weather. Pickled meat at Bloom's. 'Will somebody buy something? Otherwise I have nothing to do'

United Kingdom and Ireland

At a time when people are doing everything to make buying more and more uniform, sterile and automated, one can almost consider the blooming of the old fashioned street market as a victory for the original nature of man. Both the older and the younger generations keep on searching for the pleasant bustle and excitement of the markets so well known from olden times where one can buy anything, from fresh fruit and vegetables to new or second-hand clothes, and where one can take a look at the dealers in antiques and bric-à-brac between the weekly purchases. Just as the United Kingdom differs from the rest of Europe in essential matters, like weights and measures, so the markets differ from those on the mainland. The English have always considered the concept 'flea market' as something typical of the Continent; something that belongs to the strange manner of life that people on the other side of the Channel simply enjoy.

Rhinoceros on Portobello Road

Everyone knows what you are talking about when you talk of a flea market, but there are people who insist that the United Kingdom does not have any. Many consider the term somewhat unpleasant and distasteful and they expect that nothing can be bought at a flea market except dirty second-hand clothing. In the United States of America, the word is completely accepted as a term for a market where second-hand goods — from junk to antiques — are dealt in, without the restrictions applicable in England; it will be used in this sense in the following pages.

Until about fifteen years ago, the situation was relatively simple. In the predominantly rural provinces, the market happening was held once a week and, in the cities, daily or twice a week. Everything was on sale, from locally grown fruit and vegetables to new and used items of clothing and domestic articles which were all hopefully cheaper than at the store. Many such markets still exist and will be mentioned further on in this chapter; but there have been newer developments which have made the face of the market far more interesting.

The most important of these developments is the enormous surge in the trading of antiques in the middle and lower price brackets. Collector's fever spread rapidly and now covers a broad spectrum. Those objects which since olden times have been sought by collectors, like snuff-boxes, antique silver, fine porcelain, Art Nouveau and so on, have priced themselves out of the market. Consequently, people started collecting things like postcards, tin toys, old photographic appara-

129

ture, Art Deco and seventy-eight r.p.m. records, all of which are now offered at reasonable prices throughout the country.

Markets have always served dedicated collectors as an important source, and the increasing numbers of collectors has given rise to many new markets which then especially play up to this demand. Simultaneously, the number of dealers at the traditional mixed markets is on the increase.

Just like in any other country, the capital sets the tone: perhaps the best way to get acquainted with the flea markets of the United Kingdom is to pay a visit to a few in London.

A market is more than a place at which things are only bought and sold; a visit to one is always something exceptional. They are always sure to have an individual atmosphere. People become addicted to them in a peculiar manner and the curious person has a chance to take a look at the daily life of the local inhabitants by visiting the market. An object bought on impulse can become a valuable souvenir of the visit.

The fact that London has so many different markets does not make a delineation of their general nature particularly easy. The one extreme is the snazziness of Camden Passage and the other is the chaotic and unpredictable junk-dealers of the East End, and in between lies the terrain of those markets which comply with the wishes of the most fastidious of collectors and offer the addicted market-loungers many pleasurable hours.

If one takes a closer look at one of the most colorful and largest street markets of London, the Portobello Road, one will gather a pretty good notion of the most important characteristics of flea markets in the United Kingdom.

Like many markets, Portobello Road has expanded enormously in the last fifteen years. It became known as an antique market only at the end of the fifties. Before that, vendors sold their fruit and vegetables there, and one could also have found a few stalls with old clothes and second-hand household articles. By the end of the sixties, fashion reached an unknown climax; as a 'must' for tourists in search of 'Swinging London', only the more clothing-oriented Carnaby Street could equal Portobello Road. The market was used then as a backdrop for movies on

A professional look

'Swinging London' and so became a type of cliché. The colorful, long-haired hippies, irreverently dressed in jackets from various army units, caused a storm of protest from pensioned soldiers. Memories of those days are kept alive by the street-musicians who let *Mr. Tambourine Man* and other popular songs from the sixties resound.

Portobello Road is situated on Notting Hill, a suburb of West Central London built at the end of the nineteenth century for the benefit of the wealthy, during the reign of Queen Victoria. Nowadays, most of the large houses are being rebuilt into apartments with one or more rooms, as at the end of the fifties and beginning of the sixties, Notting Hill was definitely a dilapitated suburb. Now it has regained something of its old dignity because young and well-to-do couples are buying the smaller houses and renovating them. Thus the broad, treelined streets and pleasant squares are recovering something of their old glory.

The market itself is surprising to the visitor coming for the first time. It is most easily reached by walking from the subway station of Notting Hill along Pembridge Road to Portobello Road. At its beginning, the famous street hardly looks different from a quiet, narrow residential street with on the one side nicely painted houses

130

and on the other, one or two quiet antique shops between the houses.

But at the intersection with Chepstow Villas, the actual trade of Portobello Road suddenly begins on the Saturday morning. The entire street crawls with people, taxis keep on bringing new visitors, and stalls with silver, copper and paintings crowd the sidewalks.

Saturday is the big day for Portobello Road, which on other days looks like any other quiet London street, although there are a few stores and antique shops open in the covered gallery. But on Saturday morning, starting from seven o'clock the market vendors begin to arrive. They unload their goods from pick-ups and automobiles, and in the confusion of boxes and old newspapers, a few are busy displaying their wares on tables outside the stores; others wait for the council truck, which will bring the stalls; and still others lug their boxes one by one to the covered gallery. This is the time when the vendors do business amongst themselves and look out assiduously for new goods for their permanent customers, who will arrive later in the day.

Portobello Road stretches about a mile northwards and as one goes further, the market undergoes various metamorphoses. The very first piece is – perhaps not completely unjustifiably – known as a sort of a tourist trap, in which cheap imitations of horse-harnesses and sport-pictures are offered as the genuine article for pretty stiff prices. It appears that many visitors do not get further than the second or third side street, which is really a pity, because there is still a whole lot to be discovered all along the rest of Portobello Road, even as far as Golbourne Road, right at the most northerly point.

But the first part is undoubtedly the most colorful and attractive, and comprises, besides lesser quality goods, a number of first-class articles and the most specialized stalls of the market. That Portobello Road has unjustly been given the reputation of being pricy in some circles comes from the fact that people do not recognize the high quality of the goods. If a dealer chooses to specialize in Art Nouveau jewelry or in old musical boxes, then this does not mean that his prices have to be lower than his competitors' because he stands on Portobello Road.

Chair parked neatly on Portobello Road

Right at the beginning of Portobello Road, opposite the pink Centaur Gallery, Roger's Antique Galleries is situated. For someone who is visiting Portobello Road or whatever market in England for the first time, a look around Roger's is a good education, which makes clear much about the contemporary situation of the antique markets.

From the outside, one can see that the covered gallery is divided into separate units and that every market vendor has more or less his own speciality – silver, books and jewelry etc. It is quite impossible to judge from the outside just how extensive and comprehensive these galleries are. In fact there are some seventy-five different little stalls, and besides the more general, small antique and bric-à-brac places, there

131

Street musician on Golbourne Road

Satisfied at the Camden Lock Market

Above: *Camden Passage*

Below: *One does not buy any old how in
Camden Passage*

are vendors specialized in scientific instruments, printed pamphlets, Art Nouveau, glass-work, Eastern porcelain and other things. The antique gallery runs right through the entire width of the whole block and has an entrance in Kensington Road, which runs parallel to the Portobello Road.

It is definitely worthwhile to walk into these galleries, but also into the others, and to spend some time looking at the diverse goods on offer. Much of the excess and the large variety of Portobello Road comes through the manner in which such large galleries, and there are many of them, enlarge the density of the market and the diversity of the goods and make it possible that more than two thousand dealers can do their trade in a street which is but a mile in length.

The system of including a number of independent stalls under one roof, by which means the vendors are put into the position of doing business without the high liabilities which would cause their prices to be raised, has proved to be of inestimable importance for the small antique trade during the course of approximately the last decade. There are various people who claim that they were the first to do business in this manner, but the idea is so logical and so obvious that it is impossible to attempt to trace the originators. Covered galleries shot up like mushrooms throughout the country. Through this system, the dealers are not only able to share the fixed liabilities, but can also have a permanent place so that their customers know where and when they can be found. By displaying all their wares under a single roof, the allure for the casual passer-by is enhanced, and so dealer and customer are more than content with this method.

When the visitor has wandered around Roger's and has experienced how large a small looking place can possibly be, he will also have become aware that this also applies to the other gables, and, hopefully, at the ensuing blocks of Portobello Road – besides enjoying the more conspicuous attractions of the stalls on the street and those of the ordinary stores – he will spend his time by walking in and out of places such as 'The Corner Portobello Antique Supermarket', 'The Westbourne Antique Arcade' and 'The World Famous Portobello Market'.

Only at the corner of Westbourne Grove do the stalls known for so long begin. The market becomes even more colorful. These stalls are half as tempting as the more select stalls in the covered antique galleries but they form the essence of the challenge to go bargain-hunting; at some of the stalls, lying piled up high, are goods which at first sight really look like a 'find' but which on closer examination appear to be primarily trash; other stalls are hung full of unspectacular second-hand men's outfits, which hide from view the fascinating Victorian jewelry lying underneath.

A number of the vendors come from families which have been standing for years at the market; in the antique galleries, many of the vendors stand only temporarily. The trade in small antiques is namely a good source of extra income for writers, musicians, artists and others. At the time of the writing of this chapter, at least eighty percent of the English actors were unemployed and many of them are of the opinion that having a stall on Portobello Road is a pleasant and profitable way to spend the time between engagements. Consequently, the Portebello Road vendors always form a surprising and colorful diversity of people, who interact with one another in a most friendly manner.

Portobello Road is not an aggressive market. Usually visitors are in no way pressed by the vendors, who are usually engrossed in a book. But anyone interested in a certain article is helped cordially. A small amount of bargaining is of course expected but there is no special tradition about the difference between the initial asking price and the final sum with which the dealer agrees. For both parties this depends on intuition and experience.

Like at all antique markets, it often has little sense to bargain down the dealer's asking price; some are even irritated by this. The fixed customers and the local dealers are known to one another and can perhaps obtain better prices than a newcomer, but an incidental visitor cannot expect the same treatment. The only exception is the specialized collector whose interest and knowledge is often rewarded with a small discount on the asking price.

Foreigners are in no way at a disadvantage when buying on Portobello Road. Those who believe that an American or European accent automatically leads to a rise in price and therefore take an English friend with them to make the purchases will see that this makes no difference. Among the visitors to the market, where people of all races and nationalities crowd one another in order to select the best bargain or are only enjoying themselves, one can hear a remarkable number of foreign accents and languages. The trade keeps on going by offering antiques of good quality for reasonable prices to the visitors in the hope that they will tell their friends at home and thereby ensure a constant stream of visitors.

One of the best aids to bargaining, especially with the vendors whose stalls are outside, is the English weather. It is known that the prices drop drastically at the end of a cold, rainy afternoon. The clever visitor arrives at about eleven, walks along the stalls and casually inquires about the prices of the objects in which he is interested, without showing any enthusiasm or disapproval. After this, he takes refuge in Finch's pub named 'The Duke of Wellington', and enjoys a pleasant lunch-hour with a glass of beer and a sandwich. After whiling away the time by sauntering around two or three galleries he returns to the miserable, cold and drenched vendor who, with a bit of luck, has not sold very much and is thus comtemplating packing up and going home. This is the moment to inquire again about the price of the desired object and to begin friendly but efficacious bargaining.

It is useful to bear in mind that, despite the fact that much of the Portobello Road Market is held out of doors, a visit in bad weather is worthwhile. The vendors possess that typical English demeanor, which permits them even in the worst conditions to complain about the weather in a lively manner and this in fact heightens the friendly atmosphere. And naturally, there are sufficient covered galleries in which the visitor can find shelter while he looks around.

Like at most English markets, the pubs form a center of social activity on Portobello Road. In the summer, 'Henneky's', at the intersection of Westbourne Grove, is extremely popular because of its large beer-garden and the wide assortment of real English beer. In winter, 'The Duke of Wellington' situated on the corner of Portobello Road and Elgin Cresent, is the unavoidable

attraction where one can have a conversation and a glass of beer with the vendors and the other visitors.

The corner of Finch is something like a gathering place for street-singers, a part of Portobello Road's scene that could not be missed. One man – bands – a man who plays a guitar, a big drum strapped to his back, a tambourine on each elbow and a harmonica on his neck (and various other ingenious variations) – entertain the public on the street with the performing of all sorts of pop and folk songs. At the end of the performance, a girl goes around amiably with the hat and all contributions are welcome although they are not specifically requested.

One of the reasons that a casual visitor to Portobello Road misses the second part of the road is that after the third intersection, which can be recognized by 'The Duke of Wellington' (Elgin Crescent and Colville Terrace), the tempting assembly of paintings and bric-à-brac, old military uniforms, stuffed animals and so on suddenly merges into what looks like a completely ordinary English main road, with on both sides vegetable and fruit stalls, and after these, a diversity of supermarkets, a butcher, a material store and the inevitable 'fish and chips' store. In this section, there are also stalls with new clothes and a lively auction is often held in the middle of the road with linen or other household articles. Instead of the colorful types which one comes across on the first hundred yards of the road, one now sees the neighborhood residents behind their strollers and with bags full of shopping.

But when the visitor has worked his way through this not very exotic part, he passes under a viaduct on which a highway and the subway run, and arrives then at the Westway Market. The majority of the dealers on the Westway Market trade in goods which are of lesser quality than the dealers of the actual Portobello Road and this means that the prices are quite a bit lower.

The Westway Market originated as a reaction of the local residents to the growing popularity of the northern part of Portobello Road with its concentration of antiques. It was noticed that the result of the higher prices and the increasing

Books in Camden Passage

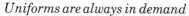

Uniforms are always in demand

specialism in antiques was that the neighborhood residents had diminishing chances of finding a place at the market. There are very long waiting-lists for standing-places at the Portobello Road Market, and there was a time when it became generally known that a site bought on the black market sometimes changed hands for two thousand dollars. Since 1972, the Westway Market is getting better all the time, and on Fridays and Saturdays, there is a market held, unlike on the northern section of Portobello Road, where one is held only on Saturdays. Stalls are easily hired and the supply of vendors outside of the permanent nucleus varies, by virtue of which there is always something new to be seen.

A part of Westway Market is 'covered', because it happens to run under the viaduct. In total, there are approximately eighty-five stalls. The reputation which Portobello Road had as a meeting-place for young people is now more applicable to Westway Market. The grubby cement walls of the viaduct along this part of the market are decorated with paintings in bright colors. When the market opened for the first time, one of the most important attractions was the free concert which was given by local rock and reggae groups under the curve in the highway. This was terminated after complaints were made about the noise, but at the Westway Market there is still music sounding from the stalls with records.

The difference between the Westway and the Portobello Road is revealled most emphatically in the stalls which are at the beginning of the former market: those which are specialized in second-hand rock and roll records; one with left-wing books and magazines; a stall full of imported African handcraft; and yet another in which all sorts of bric-à-brac is displayed, all under £5 ($12). In place of the ingenious one man-bands, which one finds in front of Finch's door, here the corner of the street is often besieged by a young, fiery Jesus freak, who attempts to persuade his contemporaries to repent.

The alternative life-style aspect of the Westway Market will not appeal to everybody but it has nevertheless become a choice place for avant-garde collectors. There are a number of stalls which specialize in decorative articles from the forties and fifties, like tea pots, bakelite radios and other things. Some of the stalls selling second-hand clothing are certainly worth closer inspection even if there are things there which one can hardly imagine anyone wanting to buy.

After the Westway Market, Portobello Road continues on towards Golbourne Road but it is here mainly a fruit, vegetable and junk market. The influence of the Westway persists until the first sidestreet where one finds many Afghani jackets and caftans. A community center provides the residents with information about housing and social security, and provides non-stop reggae music to enliven the scene. Sometimes a group of vegetarians set up a stall with vegetarian food and, in winter, the welcome attraction of a mug of hot soup. The 'Back-ah-Yard' restaurant serves West Indian food for reasonable prices and this points to the large concentration of West Indians in this part of London. Between

Negotiating at the Camden Lock Market

these establishments, the somewhat traditional seond-hand stores in furniture continue their trade.

After the intersection of Paddington and Portobello Road, the real flea market begins – old clothing and shoes lie spread out on the ground, and from a delivery van, the surplus stocks of clothes and kitchen utensils from the Ministry of War are offered for sale. This piece of Portobello Road preserves the old market tradition intact, namely leaving any unsold articles on the streets at the end of the day for whoever wants them, whether that be the garbage collector, the drunks or the insatiable bargain-hunters. It is not unusual to see a well-dressed lady looking furtively around her while she grubs about in a pile of unattended books or picks up a glass candy-dish, which is apparently still intact and has been left behind among a heap of old shoe-boxes, and lets it slide into her shopping-bag.

After a few minutes' walk, the Golbourne Road begins on one's right. It is more or less discouraging to come across such a colorless scene after the well-kept blocks of houses separated by communal gardens with trees on the other end of Portobello Road. On the left side of Golbourne Road, only fruit and vegetables are sold but on Saturdays, the right side is used for second-hand goods. These goods on sale here differ just as much from those on the northern part of Portobello Road as the surroundings do. If one has left the extravagance of the antique articles and rarities behind one, then one suddenly becomes confronted with a series of second-hand items like old hairdryers, petroleum heaters, battered television sets, sensational paperbacks and threadbare second-hand clothes. But for the persistent bargain-hunter, there are always pretty good finds to be made among what looks like junk for surprisingly low prices.

Whether one now prefers the assortment of selected antiques at the beginning of Portobello Road, where the prices vary from a few pounds to unpayable amounts, in which the price class from twenty to fifty pounds is the most common (about fifty to a hundred dollars), or rather the chaotic array of goods at Westway and Golbourne Road, where one can still purchase unusual pieces for less than a pound, is all simply a matter of personal taste or a relatively well-filled wallet. They are each entertaining in their own way: the first part is exciting to browse about and to look at in wonder, but also to get good bargains in unusual antiques and decorative pieces; the second part, by contrast, is a paradise for those who just love conjuring a pretty piece from among a pile of apparently worthless junk and purchasing it for a few pence.

The contrast between the markets at which exclusively selected antiques and jewelry are sold and those which only sell junk, persists outside of London. There are many places like Golbourne Road, where there are second-hand goods, sometimes with simple antiques amongst them, at markets which are mainly directed at agricultural and industrial produce, like fruit and vegetables, meat and fish, household articles and new clothing. This is the most usual type of market by far in the countryside and despite the fact that they do not appear very promising at first sight, they are nevertheless always lively and can be extremely pleasurable and rewarding to visit.

Those who wish to penetrate to the real heart of London's antique markets must definitely visit the 'New Caledonian Market' in Bermondsey on an early Friday morning. It was opened on its present site in 1949 after it was forced to give up the better site on which it had been situated before The Second World War, on Copenhagen Fields in Islington. The old Caledonian Market was originally established as a cattle market in 1855, even though it existed for long before that. It was a sort of mixed market where livestock was sold, agricultural produce, second-hand clothes and furniture. In the twenties, the market was closed on Tuesday and Friday mornings to livestock for the benefit of new and second-hand domestic articles and furniture, silver and other antiques. It was a lively market at which the continuous sales pitches of the vendors provided much entertainment.

It was thought that the new site in Bermondsey was chosen under the pressure of the permanent vendors because of its poor situation and lesser attractiveness. It was thought that the unfavorable situation together with the rather unpleasant opening hours (from 5:00h for small antiques and from 0:00h for the dealers to do business with one another) would put off the

incidental visitor and tourist. Whether there be any truth in this, the opposite has proved to be true, and a visit to Bermondsey in the early morning has become an unusual and often rewarding adventure for the enterprising antique collector.

Bermondsey is a rather dilapidated part of London situated on the south bank of the Thames, opposite the City of London. It is a mixture of empty storage sheds and blocks of apartments under construction. The market is held on a paved site in the open air. The atmosphere varies strongly according to the time of year: in the winter, it is very strange, almost unreal. From about four in the morning, groups of people begin assembling on the empty, tiled site. Clever dealers put tables out in the dark, while their colleagues gather in attentive groups to inspect the goods by means of flashlights. The permanent vendors of Bermondsey have succeeded in developing a clever way of hanging their flashlights around their necks or shoulders so as to have both hands free to look at the wares in these important hours while it is still dark. The lively

trade in the middle of the sleeeping city creates a scary, oppressive atmosphere.

At five o'clock, the market porters begin to bring out hand-carts with the trestles and at about half past six, the market has taken on a recognizable form with a series of long passages and tables richly covered with small antiques. One can see the dealers from the Portobello Road, the Camden Passage and the other London markets sauntering around the rows of tables, with large shopping-bags or weekend cases with them, which they gradually fill with silver, jewelry and bric-à-brac. Dealers boast that articles from Bermondsey change owners maybe a dozen times before they finally arrive at Bond Street for five or ten times the original price. These stories pop up so frequently and are so convincing that even the sceptic now believes them.

Breakfast forms a welcome break during a visit to Bermondsey in the early morning. 'Rose's Dining Rooms', in Bermondsey Street number 210, is always packed from six in the morning on with a heterogeneous group of dealers, who are busy with enormous English break-

Thousands of tourists arrive every year at Portobello Road

139

Above: *The Electric Mile, Brixton*

Below and left: *The Cutler Street Silver Market*

fasts consisting of bacon, sausages, fried eggs, fried tomatoes, beans and toast and boiling hot tea or coffee with lots of milk. The purchases are displayed in an atmosphere of friendly rivalry, and the ins and outs are discussed endlessly. An elegant gentleman in a jacket made of sheep's wool tells a long-haired cockney in denims the story of his latest book on Southern France, while two pretty girls greet a newcomer with friendly teasing. There are many old foxes in the trade among the dealers in Bermondsey and undoubtedly they know all the dodges of the antique trade. At about half past seven, the 'Hand and Marigold' pub opens up in Bermondsey Street and breakfast can be followed by a friendly glass of Guinness next to a glowing coal heater.

Despite the fact that it is fascinating to see how the market changes from nothing to something during the course of a few hours in the early morning, for the newcomer it is quite sufficient to arrive between nine and ten. At about this time, the rows of trestles are loaded with an excessive quantity of goods and the feverish trading amongst the dealers themselves ceases.

At the Caledonian Market, everything is crowded on top of everything else and the stalls are so densely filled with quality antiques that it takes about an hour before one has managed to survey the offers of the day. Despite each stall having its own appearance, they are not nearly as specialized as some of the stalls on Portobello Road. There is still a big demand for silver, but also for paintings, copper, porcelain, clocks, jewelry, decorative glasswork and curiosities. There is always an astonishing display of treasures and the quality of the actual market is, in general, high. The stalls along Bermondsey Street sell cheaper articles, from about fifty pence, but they are less interesting than the antique stalls.

Opposite the open market in Long Lane is the Bermondsey Antique Market, a covered gallery which is open on Fridays from seven to two o'clock. It is a renovated bacon factory in which a hundred and fifty stalls are housed in a strange and intricate maze of small squares and passages. The quality and style of the goods resemble that of the Portobello Road insofar as that every stand-keeper has his own limited special-

ity. Of all the covered antique galleries in London, Bermondsey is one of the most interesting and reasonably priced. Art Deco and Art Nouveau are well-represented and there is a very good stall that deals in old advertising material.

For the less adventurous, there are enough other markets in London, which are open at normal hours. One of the nicest developments in the antiques world of the last fifteen years is the opening of Camden Passage. In 1959, the surroundings of Camden Passage were very dilapidated. Since many a year, this market had been known as a second-hand market, and at the end of the fifties, markets were held in the open spaces which the bombardments had created. At the present, this market is an integrated part of London's antique trade and here both specialists in good quality antiques as well as the bric-à-brac dealers can be found.

At the peak of the summer tourist season, there are surely some sixty buses per day going to this market but even this does not destroy the unique charm. The stores and a few of the covered galleries in Camden Passage keep to the normal opening hours during the week. Camden Passage is only open to pedestrians and on Wednesdays and Saturdays, there are market stalls set up at four points along the Passage.

Whether it is because there is no traffic or because the Passage itself is so nice, Camden Passage, in comparison with other London markets, has something exceptionally peaceful about it. Many of the dealers who have a stall on the street stand there for only a part of the day and they form a far more uniform group coming from the middle classes and of middle age than the colorful and loud group of the Portobello Road. The atmosphere is very relaxed and friendly and many people applaud the absence of crowds and bustle.

The articles in the stalls form a mixture of bric-à-brac and jewelry and are usually of lesser quality than the articles in the covered galleries and stores. Nevertheless, the dealers have to comply with certain standards in order to be permitted to trade in the Camden Passage, and imitation or mass-produced primitive articles are excluded, this in favor of small antiques for normal prices. The permanent dealers come from Devon and Lancaster to stand in the Passage,

141

because of the low business costs and the constant stream of visitors.

Another attraction of Camden Passage is formed by the restaurants. 'Carrier's' at number two, and 'Frederick's' in Islington High Street number 106, deserve their name for first class food and service. Unfortunately, the prices are very high and those with more modest resources will sooner honor with their presence 'Aquilino's Bar', at Camden Passage number thirty one, or 'Portofino' at number thirty-nine, both of which serve outstanding Italian food. The 'Camden Head' at the northern end of the Passage is an extraordinarily attractive pub, which has preserved its late Victorian decor with ornate mirror glass and red velvet carpeting. This is the place where many of the dealers eat their midday meals and one can listen to the stimulating professional discussions while enjoying the traditional lunch of the English pub comprising sausages and mash, finely-chopped mutton and mash or a farmer's lunch.

There are so many specialized stalls in the Passage that the visitor will quickly find his own favorite one. The 'Georgian Village' is one of the most recently opened covered galleries and it appears that it has become very popular. It is built from designs from the York Museum and there is much authentic material from the time of George V used in the construction. Annie Moss of the 'Orange Box' just outside the 'Camden Head' is one of the most important suppliers of clothing from the period of George or Edward or other periods. 'Strike One', on the Camden Walk, has an excellent collection of old pocketwatches and clocks, and has, like many businesses in the Passage, clients from all over the world. 'Finbar McDonald' at number seventeen is specialized in pictures and among the many overseas customers belongs the White House in Washington D.C. For Art Deco enthusiasts, 'Derrick Moss', at number ten, has one of the most attractive displays in the world. And there are more.

Further past Islington High Street, opposite Camden Passage, is on Saturdays and Sundays a busy market in the morning in Chapel Street. This is predominantly a fruit and vegetable market where the residents of Islington, who form a sharp contrast with the somewhat more

Flea markets in London

- Alfie's Antique Market (covered), Church Street 13-25, Tuesday through Saturday from 10:00 to 18:00h
- Antiquarius (covered), 135-143 Kings Road, Monday through Saturday from 10:00 to 18:00h
- The Antique Hypermarket (covered), 26 Kensington High Street Monday through Saturday from 10:00 to 17:45h
- Bell Street Market, Bell Street, Saturday from 9:00 to 17:00h
- Bermondsey Indoor Antique Market (covered), 251-255 Long Lane, Friday from 5:00 to 14:00h
- Camberwell Antique Market (covered), 159-161 Camberwell Road, Thursday and Friday from 10:00 to 17:00h, Saturday from 2:00 to 18:00h
- Camden Lock Market, Chalk Farm Road, Saturday and Sunday from 9:30 to 17:30h
- Camden Passage, Upper Street, Saturday from 8:30 to 17:00h, Wednesday from 7:30 to 15:00h
- Charing Cross Collector's Market (covered), Hungerford Lane, Villiers Street, Saturday from 9:30 to 17:30h
- Chelsea Antique Market (covered), 245a and 253 Kings Road, Monday through Saturday from 10:00 to 18:00h
- Church Street Market, Church Street, Saturday from 9:00 to 17:00h
- Cutler Street Silver Market, Exchange Buildings, Cutler Street, Sunday from 8:30 to 13:00h

- Electric Mile, Electric Avenue, Saturday from 8:30 to 17:00h
- Golbourne Road Market, Golbourne Road, Saturday from 8:30 to 17:00h
- Gray's Antique Market (covered) 58 Davies Street, Monday through Friday from 10:00 to 18:00h
- Hampstead Market (covered), 12 Heath Street, Thursday from 7:00 to 17:00h
- Hoxton Street Market, Hoxton Street, Monday through Saturday from 9:00 to 17:00h
- Knightsbridge Pavillion, (covered), 112 Brompton Road, Monday through Saturday from 10:00 to 18:00h
- London Silver Vaults (covered), Chancery House, 53-63 Chancery Lane, Monday through Friday from 9:00 to 17:30h; Saturday from 9:00 to 12:30h
- The New Caledonian Market, Abbey Street, Friday from 5:30 to 15:00h
- Petticoat Lane Market, Middlesex Street, Sunday from 8:30 to 13:00h
- The Portobello Market, Portobello Road, Saturday from 8:30 to 17:30h
- Sclater Street and Cheshire Street, Sunday from 8:30 to 13:00h
- Westway Market, Portobello Road, Friday and Saturday from 8:30 to 17:30h

The numerous covered markets on Portobello Road and in the Camden Passage have not been individually mentioned

London's East
End Markets

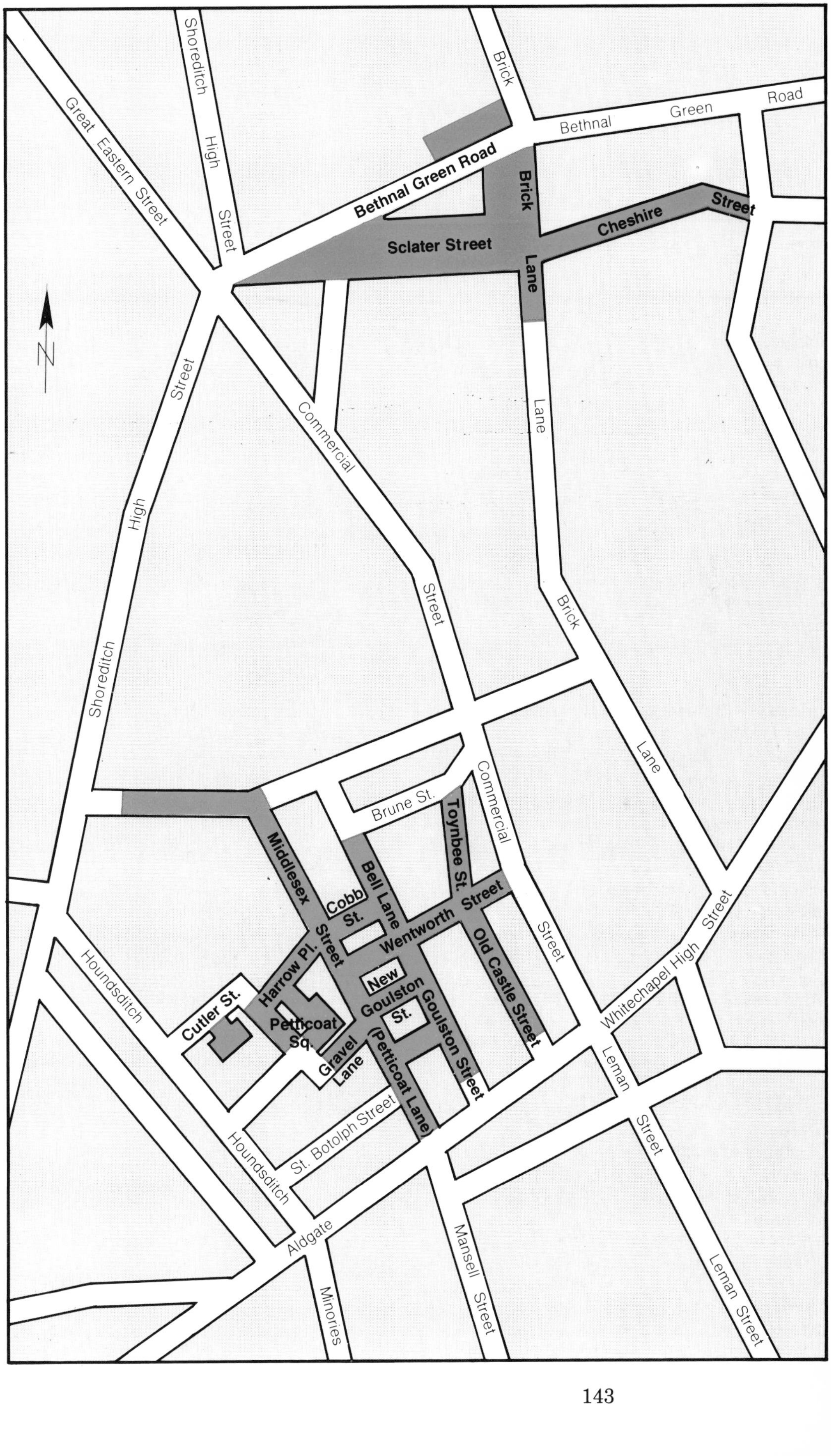

N

Shoreditch High Street

Great Eastern Street

Brick

Bethnal Green Road

Bethnal Green Road

Brick Lane

Cheshire Street

Sclater Street

Shoreditch High Street

Commercial Street

Lane

Brick Lane

Commercial Street

Brune St.

Toynbee St.

Middlesex Street

Bell Lane

Cobb St.

Wentworth Street

Old Castle Street

Whitechapel High Street

Harrow Pl.

Cutler St.

Petticoat Sq.

New Goulston St.

Goulston Street

Gravel Lane (Petticoat Lane)

Houndsditch

Leman Street

St. Botolph Street

Houndsditch

Aldgate

Minories

Mansell Street

Leman Street

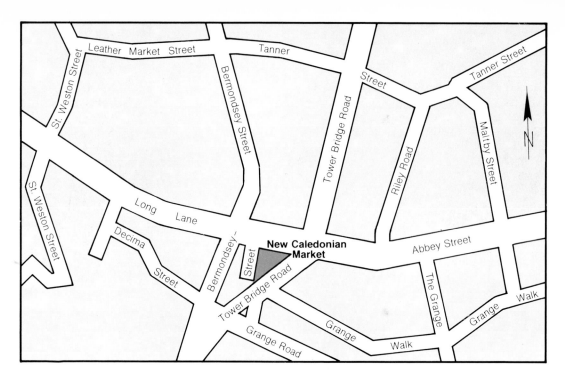

London
New Caledonian
Market

cosmpolitan clients of their purchasing.

If one considers Camden Passage as one of the newest destinations for the bus-loads of tourists, then one has to consider Petticoat Lane in London's East End as of the oldest. Petticoat Lane is a nickname given to the street-markets and covered halls in the area of Aldgate where on Sunday mornings new clothes and household articles are sold.

Before the war, Petticoat Lane was famous for its bargains in clothing (hence the name) and for its entertaining stand-workers' remarks. Again and again, the legend reappears that the goods on display were stolen – 'fallen from the back of a truck' was then the euphemism of the vendor. Newcomers were warned that they need not worry if they had lost their watch at the beginning of the alley; they would be able to re-purchase it at the end of the alley!

East End, as this neighborhood is called by the residents of London (as opposed to the modern West End: Oxford Street, Bond Street, Regent Street and Piccadilly) has always been famous for its candid, good-humored residents. The people who are born in the East End, preferable within hearing distance of Bow Bells, consider themselves to be the only genuine cockneys. The area around Aldgate has for centuries been a harbor for first-generation immigrants and there has always been a Jewish colony in this neighborhood which occupied itself with the manufacturing of ladies' and gentlemen's cloth-ing. Clothing manufactured in the East End was destined for sale in the West End and a small part of the goods from the West End appeared in a mysterious fashion in the East End for give-

Flea markets South-east England

Bromley (Kent)
● Bromley Bric-à-Brac Market, United Reformed Church Hall, Widmore Road, Thursday from 9:00 to 16:00h

Croydon (Surrey)
● Croydon Flea Market, St. Peter's Hall, Ledbury Road, Friday from 9:00 to 16:00h

Epping (Essex)
● Epping Flea Market, High Street 64-66, Saturday from 9:00 to 17:00h

Eton (Berkshire)
● Eton Antique Market, 79 High Street, Tuesday through Saturday from 10:30 to 17:30h

Hungerford (Berkshire)
● Hungerford Arcade, High Street, Monday through Saturday from 9:30 to 17:30h

Maidstone (Kent)
● Lockmeadow Market, Tuesday from 7:00 to 14:00h

Purley (Surrey)
● What Not Market, Christchurch Hall, Brighton Road, Monday from 8:30 to 15:00h

Rye (Sussex)
● Old Dairy Market, Cinque Port Street, Thursday and Saturday from 9:00 to 16:00h

Sandwich (Kent)
● Sandwich Cattle Market, Thursday from 8:00 to 15:00h

Sevenoaks (Kent)
● Antiquity, Bligh Hotel, High Street, Wednesday from 9:00 to 16:00h

Winchester (Hants)
● Antiques and Crafts Market, Kings Walk, Monday, Tuesday, Wednesday, Friday and Saturday, from 9:00 to 17:30h

Woburn (Bedfordshire)
● Woburn Abbey Antiques Centre, Monday through Saturday from 10:00 to 18:00h, Sunday from 10:00 to 17:00h

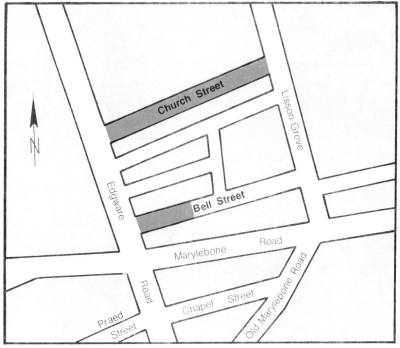

away prices; a practice which still continues.

The Jewish colony has now vanished and for the most part, many of the small tailor shops have been taken over by Indian and Pakistani immigrants, some of whose families lived for centuries in Africa. Many of the vendors are of Indian descent, something which throws visitors expecting a cockney market into confusion.

Yet 'Bloom's Restaurant', in Whitechapel High Street, a few yards from the subway station Aldgate East, is still one of the best kosher restaurants in London, both for the take-away pickled meat sandwich as well as the complete meal. The large portions and the good quality of the food make Bloom's an irresistable Sunday dinner treat for many of the visitors from the surrounding markets.

Seeing that Petticoat Lane only sells new clothing and fashion articles, there is little of interest worth buying for the flea market enthusiast. But it is still a fascinating market to simply go and take a look at. The masses of people jostling one another in the streets are always amazing.

Many of the visitors from around Petticoat Lane are not aware that a few blocks to the east, in Cheshire Street and in Sclater Street, there are markets of a completely different nature offering a large selection of second-hand goods.

Before one takes the road to Cheshire Street, it is of interest to make a quick visit to the Cutler Street Silver Market, which is situated in an out of the way courtyard named Exchange Building, just below the actual Petticoat Lane. The Sunday market begins at eight o'clock in the morning regardless of the fact that the dealers arrive somewhat earlier to do business with each other like they do at Bermondsey.

This is done in crowded doorways, along the sidewalk of Cutler Street and in groups gathered around the coffee room of an automobile in a somewhat sinister, professional atmosphere. The market is especially good for gold and silver jewelry, both antique and modern. Coins, medals and general bric-à-brac are also sold here. Large sums of money pass unexpectedly from hand to hand, and in 'Baldacci's Café', on the corner of Cutler Street, trading continues with tea and sandwiches alongside of which gold chains and twenty pound notes pass over the table.

The market area north of Petticoat Lane is at present generally known as Brick Lane Market, despite the fact that it also spans Cheshire Street, Sclater Street, Chilton Street and, if there are sufficient vendors, also the smaller side streets. As a result of renovations in the neighborhood, it has become a 'movable' market. Cheshire Street Market, for example, used to be held on the adjoining Vallance Road.

The market begins near Bethnal Green Road at the end of Sclater Street, currently known as Club Row, and has, as a result of renovations, moved back to the original terrain. The markets of Club Row and Brick Lane are much less widely known than the nearby Petticoat Lane Market. While visitors from all over London, in fact from all over the world, come to visit Petticoat Lane, Brick Lane is largely visited by residents of East End. An excursion to Brick Lane is a real Sunday family happening and most of the visitors are parents with small children, often accompanied by grandparents.

London
Church Street
Bell Street

Above left: *I'll play anything for you, from classical to modern*

Club Row is actually a market for house pets and the meeker among us ought not to venture for too long around the cages full of puppies with adorable eyes carefully recommended as terriers, or past playful kittens which plead for a friendly owner. Large white rabbits first duck away shyly and then stop to look expectantly at the passers-by, while hamsters and white mice shuffle anxiously around their cages. Birds are very popular at this market – cages with white doves, yellow parakeets are placed one upon the other in the stalls on the street. On the top floor of Sclater Street number one, enthusiastic bird lovers can find parakeets, humming birds and even toucans. Another area of interest is that of the tropical fish; one can often see proud children leaving Club Row with a new little fish in a plastic bag.

At the pet market, stalls with low-priced potted-plants quickly became part of the scene. At all the markets in the East End, one can come across 'Barney's' stalls with eels in gelatine; besides this local speciality, there are also periwinkles, mussels, shrimps, crabs, and cockles, all of them cold and served with the option of pepper

Chelsea Antique Market

Cutler Street Silver Market

Flea markets South-west England

Bath (Avon)
● Bath Antique Market, Guinea Lane, Paragon, Wednesday from 8:00 to 17:00h

Bristol
● Antique and Collector's Market, Exchange Hall, Corn Street, Friday from 9:00 to 17:00h

Chard (Somerset)
● Chard Antiques and Collector's Market, The Guildhall, Thursday from 8:00 to 16:00h

Cirencester (Gloucestershire)
● Cirencester Antiques Market, Corn Hall, Market Place, Friday from 9:00 to 15:00h

Devizes (Wiltshire)
● Devizes Open Market, Market Place, Thursday from 6:30 to 16:30h

Exeter (Devon)
● Pannier Market, St. George's Hall, Fore Street, Monday Tuesday, Thursday, Friday and Saturday from 6:00 to 17:30h, Wednesday from 6:00 to 13:00h

● Tuesday Antique Centre, 55 East Street, Tuesday from 9:00 to 17:00h

Plymouth (Devon)
● Plymouth Antique Centre, Drake Circus, Monday through Saturday, from 10:00 to 17:00h

St. Columb Major (near Newquay, Cornwall)
● Cornwall's Flea Market, The Cattle Market, Friday from 8:00 to 18:00h

Tiverton (Devon)
● Tiverton Antiques Market, 8-10 Barrington Street, daily except Thursday and Sunday from 9:00 to 17:00h

Truro (Cornwall)
● Creation Centre, Back Quay, Wednesday, Friday and Saturday, from 9:00 to 17:30h
● Premier Market, Lemon Quay, Wednesday, Friday and Saturday, from 9:00 to 17:00h

and vinegar.

Seeing that Sclater Street is a market for the local residents in a neighborhood that is far from wealthy, second-hand articles which can still possibly be used, such as old radios and television sets, teapots, glass and earthenware kitchen utensils, carpets and rugs, sewing-machines, bicycle parts and clothing gain the most attention. But amongst the second-hand goods, a modest collector can find enough in his line; this stems from the conviction of the dealers that for every object, no matter how weird, there will always be a buyer.

Besides picture postcards, there are seventy-eight r.p.m. records, old keys, well-bound books, old cameras and unusual pieces of porcelain, generally from the forties and fifties. Unlike the Westway Market, articles like the mass-produced Art Deco mantle-piece clocks, pictures with cute subjects, large decorated boards and cheese covers are not in fashion. In point of fact, these things are considered very old fashioned. In this manner, Sclater Street provides a good impression of the type of goods that one can find at the junk markets in the provinces; seeing that the people prefer buying something modern, they usually ignore all the decorative articles reminiscent of one period or another of the past. Things which are directly usable, without it being particularly noticeable that they are second-hand, are fished out eagerly.

There are two open places on the side of Sclater Street, which are worth closer inspection because of the type of goods just mentioned. The second is much larger than the first and stretches to Bacon Street and from there even as far as Brick Lane. As one gets closer to Brick Lane, the lovely display of fruit and vegetables begins to alternate with large heaps of second-hand clothing spread out on ground-sheets.

In the door-openings of Bacon Street, people continually stand selling new watches from grubby plastic shopping bags for a fraction of their store value and they are therefore constantly on the watch for the cops. The rumor does the rounds that they deliver 'on order' and if what you are interested in is not available on this Sunday, then they will have 'found' it by the next. It is exciting to see how these people melt into the crowds at a given signal on the approach

of the cops and are not longer distinguishable from the rest of the public. Their precious bags filled with watches form a harmonious whole with those of the ordinary shopping public.

Brick Lane itself is mainly a busy fruit and vegetable market and the junk searcher will have to make his way through the residents with their heavy bags full of fresh fruit and vegetables to one of the side streets a block further along Sclater Street. From the intersection with Brick Lane, Sclater Street is called Cheshire Street, and after a not very promising start of new clothes like at Petticoat Lane Market, it all transforms into a flea market. Once again, the new clothing and junk sold next to fresh fruit and vegetables is typical of the markets outside of London.

Not only are there stalls which sell articles like in Sclater Street, but there are also a number of interesting junk stores in Cheshire Street where one can find furniture, porcelain, clothing, electrical appliances, musical instruments, umbrellas and suchlike. Here, too, one will probably not find anything which is genuine antique but for somebody whose eyes start shining at the sight of a well-stocked junk store, then further investigation is irresistible.

Cheshire Street is crossed by Chilton Street and this part of the market provides a gloomy insight into the financial straits of the residents of this neighborhood. At the extreme end, close to Granby Street, there are no stalls at all but instead people, particularly older ones, stand with cases and shopping-bags full of personal possessions, which they offer for sale along the sidewalks. In the winter, a huge fire is lit and the scene reminds one of the London of Dickens rather than the London of the twentieth century.

Further along Cheshire Street, past Chilton Street, one finds all sorts of furniture sellers. Next to less interesting postwar furniture, there is a constant supply of pieces from the time of Victoria and Edward, like tables, matching chests of drawers and armchairs which are in much need of repair.

You can find the best stalls in Cheshire Street by following the narrow alleys on the right side which run to a partly covered section that looks out onto the rails which run to Liverpool Street Station. Between second-hand clothes and tools, there are also stalls with incredibly good quality Art Nouveau and Art Deco glasswork and carefully decorated clocks on marble socles, all for prices which compare favorably with those of the Portobello Road; but there are also cigarette trading-cards and Dinky Toys.

Cozy corner at the Cheshire Street Market

149

London New
Caledonian Market

Right: *Now that's a mess, at the Sclater Street Market*

The small stalls at the market in Cheshire Street continually diminish in number until finally the market comes to an end at the beginning of a new suburb where large apartment blocks, with in between the above-ground railway lines, can be seen on all sides. This city renovation stretches gradually across the entire neighborhood and replaces the streets and small houses where the market is now held. Considering that the market survived the drastic transfer from Vallance Street, it is hoped that the perseverance of the ingenuity which is typical of the London East Enders will ensure its continued existence, in whatever form that may be.

Church Street and Bell Street, old markets situated in Central London, about fifteen minutes' walk from Marble Arch, have also undergone changes recently as a result of renovations in the area; but they have survived and are in fact prospering. They are both known as a cheap source of second-hand furniture and other objects, with once in a while, an odd antique appearing. They are both open on Saturday. Despite their being less entertaining and less

Just a corner on Portobello Road

Flea markets East Anglia and West Midlands

East Anglia
Acle (Norfolk)
● Main A47 Road, Thursday from 9:15 to 15:00h, auction from 12:00h

Bury St. Edmonds (Suffolk)
● The Market, Cornhill, Wednesday and Saturday from 8:00 to 18:00h

Fakenham (Norfolk)
● Fakenham Flea Market, The Corn Hall, Thursday from 8:30 to 15:30h, auction from 11:00h

Huntingdon (Cambridgeshire)
● Kimbolton Antique Market, Cromwell House, Kimbolton, Tuesday through Sunday from 10:00 to 17:30h

Norwich (Norfolk)
● Cloisters Antique Market, St. Andrew's Hall, George Street, Wednesday from 10:00 to 16:00h

Swaffham (Norfolk)
● Market Place, Saturday from 8:00 to 18:00h

West Midlands
Birmingham
● St. Martin's Retail (Rag) Market, Edgbaston Street, Tuesday, Friday and Saturday from 11:00 to 17:00h; Monday from 7:30 to 14:00h (only antiques)
● Stratford House Antiques Market, St. Peter's Place, Broad Street, Thursday from 8:00 to 17:00h, Sunday from 10:30 to 13:30h

Stoke on Trent (Staffordshire)
● Hanley General Market, Market Square, Hanley, Wednesday, Friday and Saturday, from 8:00 to 17:00h

Wolverhampton (West Midlands)
● Bilston Open Market, Market Street, Bilston, Monday, Friday and Saturday, from 8:00 to 18:00h

extensive than Portobello Road, they have the advantage of being cheaper.

At the intersection with Edgeware Road, Bell Street is first a fruit and vegetable market and new clothing market, but after a few of these stalls, it changes into a flea market. The number of stalls varies with the weather and particularly these dealers are inclined to pack up and go home if there is not much business going. There are certainly also other interesting stores in this street. For example, Bell Galleries, at the end of Edgeware Road, sells unpretentious second-hand furniture and articles for prices ranging from one to ten pounds. In the stalls one finds pieces of porcelain, mass-made Art Deco, ivory and mother-of-pearl jewelry, small silver items and old lace and linen table cloths.

Further on in the street, it seems as if the furniture has got the upper hand both in the stores as well as in the stalls. 'The Trap', at number forty-eight, is specialized in copper cribs, natural firewood dressing tables and crates; at number fifty, one can find interesting pieces for decoration hidden among the stools and electric heaters. Number eighty-three and eighty-seven both sell interesting second-hand books.

Five minutes' walk along Edgeware Road one arrives in Church Street, which runs parallel to Bell Street. This market is larger than that of Bell Street and is usually busier and rowdier as a result of people being attracted by low-priced clothing, fresh fruit and vegetables in the first part of the street. The extension of this market for fruit and articles of use, since the renovations, has driven the dealers onto the street but second-hand goods and antiques still form an important part of the end of Church Street near Lisson Grove.

A new covered gallery, called 'Alfie's', from numbers thirteen to twenty-five, indicates the start of the junk and antique market. One of the best stalls in the street is situated opposite to 'Alfie's'. There carpets are sold, from ordinary hearth rugs to Persian carpets, all for very reasonable prices. 'Ol' Texas', at number thirty-six, is one of the most colorful figures in the street, with his cowboy clothing and his so-called Texan accent. He calls the store 'Ol' Texas Sells Ol' Things', sounds very simple, but whoever attempts to buy any 'ol' thing' from him will in

almost all probability discover that he has incidentally chosen a piece of 'antique', which is consequently of an inevitably higher price.

On the corner of Lisson Grove is a Saturday market with twelve stalls squeezed onto a few square yards. Carefully selected pices of porcelain, glass, silver, jewelry and bric-à-brac are displayed. The prices are reasonable and the atmosphere is pleasantly casual. Constant bargaining, like in the junk stores, is not necessary here.

The place for which one can always head for good quality antiques is 'Alfie's Antique Market'. This is a relatively new establishment in Church Street, having been opened in 1976. One will find within a hundred and fifty stands and a cafetaria. Similar covered galleries for antiques are sprouting throughout the entire country as a reaction to the continually increasing demand for small antiques and decorative articles in the middle price range.

Camden Passage and Portobello Road have a number of covered galleries for antiques, as has been already pointed out. The rest of the most important galleries in London and those in the countryside are mentioned in the lists below and are marked with a black dot before their names.

Customers are undoubtedly benefited by the covered antique galleries because of the union of a number of small dealers under one roof. Some of them even accept credit cards and travellers' checks, which implies that one need not even carry cash any longer, something risky but until recently, the usual manner of affairs at street markets. The best of the antique galleries are fascinating to visit and quite often provide the client with new and creative ideas. They are included in this survey of flea markets because they have become an important and suitable source of the type of object which one may look for at a flea market, despite the fact that no one would presume to suggest that these galleries possess the same pleasant tension and atmosphere as the well known street markets.

The new Camden Lock Market, open on Saturdays and Sundays, forms the mean between the easy comfort of the covered galleries and the confused junk of the more traditional street market. During the last four years, this market has constantly increased in size, and is now one

Flea markets North-west England, East Midlands, Yorkshire and Humberside, North England

North-west England
Chester
● Chester Antique Market, Guildhall, Watergate Street, Thursday from 9:00 to 15:00h

Liverpool
● Garston Market, Island Road South, Garston, Tuesday and Friday from 8:00 to 18:00h
● North General Market, Great Homer Street, Saturday from 9:00 to 17:00h
● St. Martin's Market, Great Homer Street, Monday, Tuesday, Thursday, Friday and Saturday, from 9:00 to 17:00h, Wednesday from 9:00 to 13:00h

Manchester
● Butter Lane Antiques Market, 10A King Street West, Monday through Saturday from 9:30 to 17:00h

Preston (Lancashire)
● Retail Market, Earl Street, Lancaster Road, Monday, Wednesday, Friday and Saturday from 7:30 to 18:00h

East Midlands
Alford (Lincolnshire)
● Market Square, Tuesday from 8:00 to 14:00h, auction at 12:00h

Derby
● The Flea Market, East Street, Saturday from 9:00 to 17:00h
● Sneinton Retail Market, Bath Street, Monday and Saturday from 9:00 to 13:00h

Yorkshire and Humberside
Halifax (Yorkshire)
● Antique & Collector's Market, Piece Hall, Friday from 9:00 to 17:00h

Sheffield (South Yorkshire)
● Antique & Collector's Market, The Setts Market, Exchange Street, Monday from 9:00 to 17:30h

Skipton (Yorkshire)
● Antique & Collector's Market, High Street, Sunday from 10:00 to 17:00h

North England
Carlisle (Cumbria)
● Covered Market, Scotch Street, Monday through Saturday from 7:30 to 17:30h

Wales

Abergavenny (Gwent)
- Open Market, Tuesday from 10:00 to 15:00h

Aberystwyth (Dyfed)
- Sunday Market, Sunday from 10:00 to 16:00h

Brecon (Powys)
- The Provision Market, Friday from 9:00 to 17:30h

Cardiff
- Cardiff Antique Fayre, Mill Lane, Tuesday and Saturday from 9:00 to 17:30h

Carmarthen (Carmarthenshire)
- Market Pavilion, Wednesday and Saturday from 9:00 to 17:30h

Llandudno (Gwynedd)
- General Market, Monday, Tuesday, Thursday and Friday, from 9:00 to 17:00h, Wednesday from 9:00 to 13:00h

Llanelli (Dyfed)
- Market Hall, Thursday and Saturday from 9:00 to 17:00h

Llanidloes (Powys)
- General Market, Saturday from 9:00 to 17:00h

Machynlleth (Powys)
- Retail General Market, Maengwyn Street, Wednesday from 9:00 to 17:30h

Monmouth (Gwent)
- Produce Market, Friday and Saturday from 9:00 to 17:00h

Neath (West Glamorgan)
- Market Hall, Wednesday and Saturday from 9:00 to 17:00h

Newport (Gwent)
- General Retail Market, Saturday from 10:00 to 16:30h

Pontypridd (Glamorgan)
- Retail Market, Wednesday and Saturday from 9:00 to 17:00h

Pwllheli (Gwynedd)
- Open Air Market, Wednesday from 9:00 to 17:30h

Swansea (Glamorgan)
- Swansea Market, Oxford Street, daily except Sunday from 9:00 to 17:00h, Thursday from 9:00 to 13:00h

Tenby (Dyfed)
- Retail Market, daily except Sunday from 9:00 to 17:30h, Wednesday from 9:00 to 13:00h

Wrexham (Clwyd)
- Eagles Meadow Open Market, Monday from 9:00 to 17:30h

Scotland

Aberdeen (Grampian)
- Market Street, Monday through Saturday 8:30 to 18:00h

Ayr (Strathclyde)
- Afflecks Auction Rooms & Sales, Nile Court, High Street, Monday through Saturday from 9:30 to 16:30h, auction Tuesday at 10:00h

Edinburgh (Lothian)
- Greyfriars Market, Forrest Road, Monday through Saturday from 9:00 to 18:00h
- Royal Highland Market, Ingliston, Sunday from 10:00 to 16:00h

Glasgow (Strathclyde)
- Glasgow's Victorian Village, 67 West Regent Street, Monday through Friday from 10:00 to 17:00h, Saturday from 10:00 to 16:00h
- The Barrows, near Barrowland Ballroom, London Road, Gallowgate, Saturday and Sunday from 9:00 to 13:00h

Kilmarnock (Strathclyde)
- Open Air Market, West Langland Street, Thursday and Saturday from 10:00 to 16:30h

Laurencekirk (Grampian)
- Auction Mart, Monday from 9:00 to 16:00h

Perth (Tayside)
- Castlegate Market, Friday from 9:00 to 13:00h

of the most popular, especially among young people, who form the largest share of the vendors and fixed clientele. Part of the attractiveness of the market lies in the pleasant attitude of the vendors, who evoke the impression that they do what they do because they enjoy it and that they consider a chat with the customer just as important as doing hard business.

The market is situated in the north of Central London on a small site between a railroad bridge and a canal. In the summer, the canal is an unexpected oasis and it is possible to walk along its banks to Regent's Park and to the London Zoo. The ship owners of 'Jenny Wren' provide boat trips in barges for the less energetic. In the winter, it can look pretty grim and the surrounding streets appear to be dreary and dilapidated; but the market itself always offers a lively appearance.

Right near the entrance is a small food stall and the delicious aroma of chili con carne and fried sausages rises into the air. All the food is take-away and so can be eaten standing along the side of the market; the home-made dishes are heartily recommended! Most dishes cost under the fifty pence. Behind the food stall is 'The Black Shed', the covered section of the market, which besides its choice of art products and second-hand goods can also boast of a palm-reader. Throughout the market, the goods for sale, a mixture of good quality art and antiques in the lower price bracket – second-hand clothing and shoes from different periods, jewelry which belongs with a certain outfit, buttons, seventy-eight r.p.m. records and advertising material – are well-represented in well-selected collections. The artistic section comprises everything from macramé plant-hangers to silver jewelry, suitcases, patchwork and earthenware. The best dealers in art succeed in living entirely from their trade by selling complete stocks during the weekends and by then making articles to order during the week; they swear unanimously that they do better business at Camden Lock than at any other place.

Behind the market itself is a pleasant courtyard with workshops on the banks of the canal, where earthenwork, ceramics and burned glass are sold on the spot. 'Le Routier Restaurant', opposite these workshops, has a fine French kitchen and the prices are reasonable. In 'Dingwall's Dance Hall', London's promising orchestras as well as the good ones perform in the evenings for an enthusiastic public.

To end the reconnaisance of this area, it is necessary to leave the market and to walk under the railroad bridge on to Chalk Farm. On the right hand side of the road there are diverse stores with second-hand goods for relatively cheap prices. At times, dealers come with delivery vans from which they then sell used household apparature. During market hours, there is on the left side a hall bearing the name 'Warehouse Number Eight', with approximately three hundred and sixty square yards of antiques and bric-à-brac, which is open to visitors.

Portobello Road, Camden Passage and the New Caledonian Market are the three largest markets for antiques, and, as appears from the above descriptions, they each have their own character so that there is something for everybody. The markets of the East End offer color and bustle and one can, on the odd occasion, make a real good find amongst the bric-à-brac. Church Street and Bell Street are easily reached, while Camden Lock provides an opportunity for an excursion to a market which is diversified in its display of both contemporary ornaments as well as items from the past. The covered antique galleries, which keep on sprouting out of the ground, offer the possibility of seeing the 'crème de la crème' of all the markets without the discomfort of trips through the unpredictable English weather but also without the eventful aspect which a street market usually affords.

It has not been possible to mention all of London's markets; it is up to the reader to make a choice from the accompanying lists. Some street markets have been mentioned rather as a result of their atmosphere and surrounding streets with interesting stores than because of the wares or the market itself. But each market requires a different approach from a different point of view.

In the rest of the United Kingdom, the markets differ according to the regions in which they are situated. Normally, the combination of fruit and vegetables and second-hand articles is the ordinary picture, like on Golbourne Road or at the markets of the East End; but some of the larger cities, like Liverpool or Birmingham, have markets which only sell antiques and second-hand goods. In the more densely populated areas, more and more covered galleries are being established.

In rural areas, like in parts of Wales, Scotland and East Anglia, the markets meet the requirements primarily of the farmers in the district and are often held at the cattle-market itself. At a few markets in some small towns in the outlying regions, such as are mentioned below, the times of the auctions are also given; this is a result of the habit of selling second-hand articles rather by means of an auction than through a dealer. The auctioneer sells things like wood, chickenwire, agricultural machinery, fresh fruit and vegetables, but also ordinary furniture and bric-à-brac. These markets can be a real source of bargains but they require patience and a discerning eye in order to be able to pick out that forgotten piece of antique from a pile of trash.

In Ireland, there still exists a network of ambulatory dealers. They travel from one city to the next to sell their goods at the weekly markets for vegetables, fruit and cattle. London dealers regularly comb the Irish Republic and Ulster in search of antiques, so those who expect to venture into virgin market territory to look for bargains will be disillusioned. But it is still quite possible to make good buys, although long negotiating as to price and value of an article under consideration is strictly necessary.

The 'Sneinton Retail Market' in Nottingham, an industrial city in the Midlands with a population of 300,000, is rather typical of the English provincial market. As is often the case, the market has been driven by renovations in the city from the picturesque but rather impractical site on which it was held before the war. The market is now situated on a bricked, triangular open site just outside the center of the city; but on Mondays and Saturdays, it is still held next to the Sneinton Wholesale Market.

The stalls are set up in rows with the rear sides against one another and the vendors keep the public occupied with loud recommendations of their goods. 'The best bananas are only twenty pence per pound here.' At the Saturday market, the children also do their share of the work and they have adopted exactly the same intonation of

155

the vendors; they round off all their transactions with the line, 'thank you very much sweetie'.

The visitors to the market, mainly from Nottingham and the surrounding areas, come to stock up on fresh fruit and vegetables and to take a critical look at the household and clothing items, desirous of a good deal. Approximately thirty percent of the stalls sell second hand things – an assortment of decorative bric-à-brac and second-hand clothing and shoes, all most useful. Just like at the mixed markets of London, there is very little demand for decorative pieces from the residents. Therefore the visitor can often lay his hands on attractive porcelain or glass, or on old jewelry and pocket-watches, all for extremely competitive prices. Stalls with books and old comic strips offer the possibility of finding something good in the provinces for a fraction of the London prices.

Opposite the Sneinton Market is Bath Street, with on both sides stores selling second-hand goods. It is especially in these places, that do not particularly sell antiques, that the visitor can often find good bargains. In this category, the tendency exists to value differently the goods in the different parts of the country, while with the genuine antiques in the hands of professional dealers, the spontaneous tendency is to stick to the national price-index. The stores in Bath Street deal in complete household inventories; in between the kitchen cupboards and the three-piece suits, a genuine piece of forgotten antique silver or an old painting may pop up.

Some cities have a street market where only second-hand articles and antiques are sold for reasonable prices, usually on Saturday morning. The last section of Gardner Street in Brighton is a good example of this and demonstrates also how important it is that one knows where to go. The pre-eminent market in Brighton, called the Open Market, where only fruit, vegetables and groceries are sold is simply a bore. Visitors in search of antiques will most probably be referred to the city section named 'The Lanes' consisting of a series of narrow picturesque streets which run along the side of a hill. 'The Lanes', as far as architecture goes, are interesting – with their Georgian gables which have hardly been altered since the end of the eighteenth century – and have some of the best restaurants in Brighton.

Their snazzy antique stores have a long-standing reputation for being expensive, despite the fact that many, as is usual in such cases, will deny it.

Upper Gardner Street is only ten minutes' walk from The Lanes but is situated in a less classy area of the city behind the famous Royal Pavilion, where simple little houses with communal gardens stand on both sides of the hilly road. It is a fine neighborhood for junk stores and ordinary antique shops but on Saturday morning, the market forms the main attraction. From about half past eight, the vendors in second-hand wares begin to spread out their articles on trestles, which are set up in front of the peaceful-looking houses. On market days, the street is closed to traffic and the atmosphere is, all in all, more relaxed than that in London, and some dealers only arrive at half past ten or eleven in order to claim their sites.

Generally speaking, the dealers of the Upper Gardner Street are older and more sedate than their London counterparts and are much easier in their intercourse. There is one that does good business by displaying the few good articles which he has on the main table and by making it known that the articles on the side tables all cost fifty pence and everything in the boxes only ten pence. The response among the incidental passers-by is so good that one wonders how come this system is not more widespread.

The goods in Upper Gardner Street fall into a low price category, varying from one to ten pounds. The articles are all really 'old', at least there are no flaunting displays of imitation copper and pictures in frames such as one finds often at the more tourist-oriented markets; but where there are genuine antiques, they are usually of an inferior quality.

Visitors to the Upper Gardner Street are mainly the residents of Brighton and there is a remarkable understanding between market-vendors and the permanent customers. Small groups of people stand together in the middle of the street to exchange the latest bits of gossip. Young couples are not only attracted to come and live in these streets but also students from the nearby university and the surrounding suburbs. The sellers approach a passer-by in a friendly fashion without being too familiar, like the market-woman once did to the dozen odd people inspecting her wares in the stall: 'Will somebody please buy something, otherwise I have nothing to do.' This appeared to prick the consciences of the people and a stream of purchases followed.

Such incidents occur regularly at British and Irish markets. Each markets has been mentioned for its particular character, and they offer, besides the charm of the goods on sale, an insight into the temperament of the daily life of the local community.

The retail trade has done its best to utterly overshadow the ancient markets, by seeing to a supply of packaged, pre-washed vegetables, and an endless amount of guarantees and continuously more ingenious credit card systems and customer baits. Yet nobody can wipe out the appeal of the good old-fashioned market. They bloom on the cobblestones for the simple reason that people really like them and it looks as if it is going to stay that way.

The remains of the market are swept up

Flea markets Northern Ireland (Ulster)

Aldergrove (Co. Antrim)
● Sunday Market, Nutt's Corner, Sunday from 9:00 to 13:00h

Ballygowan (Co. Down)
● The Antique Market, Comber Road, Monday through Saturday, from 9:30 to 17:00h

Ballymena (Co. Antrim)
● Ballymena Market, Saturday from 9:00 to 13:00h

Bangor (Co. Down)
● Bangor Market, Wednesday from 9:00 to 13:00h

Belfast
● Belfast Variety Market, May Street, Friday from 9:00 to 13:00h
● Smithfield Market, Smithfield Square, daily except Sunday from 9:00 to 17:00h, Wednesday from 9:00 to 13:00h

Enniskillen (Co. Fermanagh)
● Enniskillen Market, Thursday from 9:00 to 13:00h

Jonesboro (Co. Armagh)
● Jonesboro Sunday Market, Sunday from 9:00 to 13:00h

Larne (Co. Antrim)
● Larne Market, Wednesday from 9:00 to 13:00h

Lurgan (Co. Armagh)
● Lurgan Market, Wednesday from 9:00 to 13:00h

Portadown (Co. Armagh)
● Portadown Market, Saturday from 9:00 to 13:00h

Warrenpoint (Co. Down)
● Sunday Market, Sunday from 9:00 to 13:00h

See you later, market

Flea markets Irish Republic

Cork
● Cork Antique Market, 9 Tuckey Street, Friday and Saturday from 10:30 to 18:00h
● Coal Quay Market, Cornmarket Street, Friday and Saturday from 10:00 to 17:00h
● Kasbah Market, Emmet Place, Saturday and Sunday from 9:00 to 16:00h

Dublin
● Dandelion Market, 131A St. Stephen's Green West, Saturday and Sunday from 10:00 to 18:00h

● Iveagh Market, Francis Street, Thursday through Saturday from 9:00 to 18:00h
● Johnny Giles' Dublin Bazaar, Hanbury Lane, Meath Street, Saturday from 10:00 to 17:30h
● Phoenix Park Market, Phoenix Park Racecourse, Castleknock, Sunday from 11:30 to 17:00h

Galway
● Eyre Square Market, Monday through Saturday from 10:00 to 18:00h

158

Register

I.G.Domingo, S.A. BARCELONA-SPAIN D.L.B-35.099-81